SCIENTIFIC AMERICAN EXPLORES BIG IDEAS

Science's Greatest Myths

Published in 2026 by Scientific American Educational Publishing
in association with **The Rosen Publishing Group**
2544 Clinton Street, Buffalo NY 14224

Contains material from Scientific American®, a division of Springer Nature America, Inc., reprinted by permission, as well as original material from The Rosen Publishing Group®.

First Edition

Scientific American
Lisa Pallatroni: Project Editor

Rosen Publishing
Andrea Davison-Bartolotta: Compiling Editor
Michael Moy: Senior Graphic Designer

Cataloging-in-Publication Data

Names: Scientific American, Inc.
Title: Science's greatest myths / edited by the Scientific American Editors.
Description: Buffalo, New York : Scientific American Educational Publishing, an imprint of Rosen Publishing, 2026. | Series: Scientific American explores big ideas | Includes glossary and index.
Identifiers: ISBN 9781538313077 (pbk.) | ISBN 9781538313084 (library bound) | ISBN 9781538313091 (ebook)
Subjects: LCSH: Errors, Scientific–Juvenile literature. | Discoveries in science–Juvenile literature. | Science–History–Juvenile literature.
Classification: LCC Q172.5.E77 S356 2026 | DDC 509–dc23

Manufactured in the United States of America
Websites listed were live at the time of publication.

Cover: Heartland Arts/Shutterstock.com

CPSIA Compliance Information: Batch # CSSA26.
For Further Information contact Rosen Publishing at 1-800-237-9932.

CONTENTS

INTRODUCTION

There are many widely accepted scientific ideas that, upon closer examination, reveal themselves to be oversimplifications or even outright myths. The process of scientific discovery is far from perfect, and such myths have often found their way into popular understanding, distorting the complexities of the natural world.

This book aims to highlight and challenge some of the most prevalent misconceptions that have shaped how we think about science and the universe. Section One, "Wild Whispers: Animal Myths Unveiled," looks at at animal myths big and small (just like the animals themselves!). Section Two, "Myth and Mystery Within Us," is a grouping of articles about all about the human body. Do we really only use 10% of our brain? Read on to find out!

In Sections Three and Four, the articles touch on topics such as weather and general science. Is it true that tornadoes (and toilet water) spin in the opposite direction in the Southern Hemisphere? Can we really bring animals back from extinction?

Section Five, "Food Fallacies," is a selection of articles that challenges some of our beliefs about food and how we prepare, eat, and utilize the food around us. Section Six–"Our People and Planet"–includes articles about commons myths we might hold on to about our planet and the people who live on it. Finally, Section Seven is a grouping of articles that are all opinion pieces that have been published by Scientific American.

The collection of articles in this book invites readers to think critically about the science they encounter every day. Each one challenges the assumption that everything labeled as scientific is automatically true, encouraging skepticism and curiosity. As we journey through these common misconceptions, we learn that science is as much about asking the right questions as it is about finding the right answers.

Section 1: Wild Whispers: Animal Myths Unveiled

Is the Alpha Wolf Idea a Myth?

By Stephanie Pappas

If you've ever heard the term "alpha wolf," you might imagine snapping fangs and fights to the death for dominance. The idea that wolf packs are led by a merciless dictator is pervasive, lending itself to a shorthand for a kind of dominant masculinity.

But it turns out that this is a myth, and in recent years wildlife biologists have largely dropped the term "alpha." In the wild, researchers have found that most wolf packs are simply families, led by a breeding pair, and bloody duels for supremacy are rare.

"What would be the value of calling a human father the alpha male?" says L. David Mech, a senior research scientist at the U.S. Geological Survey, who has studied wolf packs in the wild for decades. "He's just the father of the family. And that's exactly the way it is with wolves."

Family Packs

Mech, like many wildlife biologists, once used terms such as alpha and beta to describe the pecking order in wolf packs. But now they are decades out of date, he says. This terminology arose from research done on captive wolf packs in the mid-20th century—but captive packs are nothing like wild ones, Mech says. When keeping wolves in captivity, humans typically throw together adult animals with no shared kinship. In these cases, a dominance hierarchy arises, Mech adds, but it's the animal equivalent of what might happen in a human prison, not the way wolves behave when they are left to their own devices.

In contrast, wild wolf packs are usually made up of a breeding male, a breeding female and their offspring from the past two or three years that have not yet set out on their own—perhaps six to 10 individuals. In the late 1980s and 1990s Mech observed a pack every year at Ellesmere Island in northeastern Canada. His study, published in 1999 in the *Canadian Journal of Zoology*, was among the first multiyear research on a single pack over time. It revealed that all members of the pack defer to the breeding male and that, regardless of sex or age, all pack members besides that male defer to the breeding female. The youngest pups also submit to their older siblings, though when food is scarce, parents feed the young first, much as human parents might tend to a fragile infant.

The same is true across gray wolf packs: Infighting for dominance is basically unheard of in a typical pack. When offspring are two to three years old, they leave the pack in search of mates, aiming to start their own pack. The alpha wolf notion of challenging dad for dominance of the existing pack just isn't in the wolf playbook.

Indeed, even general family conflict is rare, Mech says. "Let's say that [a] pair has some yearling wolves that haven't dispersed yet. The adults will kind of keep the yearlings away from the carcass while the adults feed and feed the pups," he says. "Those are places where there can be at least competition and sometimes conflict, but it's a snap or two."

Mech used the alpha wolf nomenclature in a classic book of wolf biology, *The Wolf: Ecology and Behavior of an Endangered Species*, which was published in 1970. But he has made a point of pushing back against the term as new research has come to light. After a years-long effort, he finally got The Wolf taken out of print in 2022, he says. The 2003 book *Wolves: Behavior, Ecology, and Conservation*, which he co-edited with zoologist Luigi Boitani, is now far more accurate and up-to-date, he says.

Unusual Cases

On rare occasions wolf packs do balloon in size. This happens in Yellowstone National Park, where there are copious elk and multiple large wolf packs. Sometimes young wolves stay with their birth pack because there is enough food to go around and dispersing is dangerous. Any wolf ready to strike out on its own is at risk of attack by neighboring packs, says David Ausband, a wolf researcher and wildlife biologist at USGS and the University of Idaho. "When density is high, it's a gauntlet," he says. "It's like, 'I'll just stay home. At least I'll get some food.'"

In these situations, packs may grow to a couple of dozen members strong. The Druid Peak wolf pack in Yellowstone reached an apex of an unprecedented 37 wolves in 2001, according to the Yellowstone Wolf Tracker. When such an increase occurs in a pack, there may be more than one breeding pair, and competition can erupt over breeding spots, Ausband says. "In that case, I personally think the alpha term applies because there is still a dominant female calling the shots in that pack," he says. "Usually the second breeding female is her daughter." (In these circumstances, a subordinate male will also take on a breeding role, though sometimes one dominant male mates with multiple breeding females. Wolves rarely inbreed unless they are in small, isolated populations, so this arrangement is most likely if an unrelated female joins the pack.)

Having multiple breeding pairs in a pack is now an uncommon situation, says Ausband, who conducts genetic studies to understand how wolf packs are related and how they disperse. Prior to human hunting and trapping of the gray wolf population in the northern Rocky Mountains, perhaps 10 to 15 percent of wolf packs in the population had multiple breeders. Since the intermittent legalization of hunting and trapping of these wolves in states around Yellowstone in 2009, Ausband has found only one instance of such an arrangement in Idaho.

The status of gray wolves is often in flux. In 2008 the U.S. Fish and Wildlife Service removed the northern Rocky Mountain population from the Endangered Species Act list. The agency reinstated this population to the list that same year but then delisted it, outside of wolves in Wyoming, in 2009, allowing hunting and trapping for the first time in decades. These wolves were reinstated in 2010 and then delisted again in 2011. Northern Rocky Mountain wolves in Wyoming were subsequently delisted in 2012, relisted in 2014 and delisted again in 2017. As of a February 2022 court order, all gray wolves in the continental U.S. and Mexico outside of the northern Rocky Mountain population are protected from hunting and trapping under the Endangered Species Act.

Hunting and trapping may also reshuffle wolf families, depending on which member of the pack is killed. Breeding males and females tend to be older and less susceptible to error in their survival instincts, so it's usually younger wolves that lose their lives, Mech says. But if a breeding female or male is killed, a lone dispersing wolf may step in to take its place. On other occasions, a pack may adopt a lone wolf that does not become a breeder, says Sarah Bassing, a postdoctoral researcher at the University of Idaho and the Idaho Cooperative Fish and Wildlife Research Unit. This may happen when hunting and trapping cause a lot of wolf mortality, Bassing says, though the evidence isn't entirely clear. If a wolf pack loses too many hunting adults, it may simply need the extra help. "Packs might be more receptive to new individuals just so their pups survive to the next year," Bassing says. A spare nonbreeding adult can help guard pups and hunt for food.

Nevertheless, Bassing says, there seems to be a lot of variability across regions in how wolf packs respond to human meddling. Decades after researchers came to mistaken conclusions about wolf dynamics by studying captive animals, it's still not entirely clear how human actions are affecting how packs work. "There's a lot we don't know about how hunting and tracking tinkers with pack structure," Ausband says.

About the Author

Stephanie Pappas is a freelance science journalist based in Denver, Colo.

Males Aren't Larger Than Females in Most Mammalian Species

By Rachel Nuwer

In *The Descent of Man*, Charles Darwin posits that in most species of mammals, males are larger than females. Although Darwin did not cite evidence to back up this claim, his view on sexual size dimorphism was readily accepted as fact, and it still dominates today.

But Darwin, in this case, seems to have been wrong. An analysis of 429 mammalian species published in *Nature Communications* reveals that just 45 percent feature males that are larger than females. Nearly an equal number of species, 39 percent, have sexes that are about the same size. And in 16 percent of species, females are larger than males.

"There's been this really strong inertia toward the larger male narrative, but it was just based on Darwin's hand-wavy statement, and the evidence doesn't really support it," says the study's lead author Kaia Tombak, a postdoctoral evolutionary biologist at Purdue University. That this narrative has endured for so long "may reflect Western societal biases that tend to look at issues through a male lens."

Tombak found herself conducting the new study by chance after she and some other researchers in an online seminar began debating the factors that shape male and female aggressiveness in species whose sexes are the same size. No one knew the answer, so Tombak decided to look into it. But she quickly realized she'd have to deal with another problem first: a lack of reliable data about how many species actually have males and females of the same size. Her hunt for answers turned into a nearly three-year-long "COVID passion project," she says, which she conducted during her previous position as a postdoc at Hunter College of the City University of New York.

Most past studies that compared male and female size, Tombak found, only considered the average body mass for each of the sexes.

The authors then drew conclusions based on whatever cutoff they set for determining if there was a difference. "It was just arbitrary," Tombak says. Virtually all of these papers reinforced Darwin's view that males are larger than females in mammalian species.

Tombak and her colleagues did find one paper that clearly bucked the trend in terms of the conclusions its author came to: a study from 1976 by biologist Katherine Ralls. She looked at size patterns across mammalian taxa and found that most species did not exhibit extreme sexual size dimorphism and that larger females were surprisingly common as well. Her findings, however, were frequently either overlooked or misconstrued, Tombak says. "By then, the narrative about larger males had been around for 100 years, so it kept going," she adds.

Tombak and her colleagues started filling in the gaps by conducting a thorough literature review, oftentimes turning to "obscure" papers published decades ago, she says. They were looking for not just averages pertaining to the sexes' sizes but also measures of variance around the mean so they could apply statistical tests to determine whether a species truly seemed to be dimorphic.

Most past research on this topic has also been biased toward charismatic species such as carnivores, primates and ungulates, Tombak found. She and her colleagues corrected for this by sampling 5 percent of species across each of 16 mammalian orders that contained at least 10 species each, groups that ranged from bats to rodents. They also sampled 3.8 percent of species in an additional order, Eulipotyphla, which includes moles, shrews and hedgehogs.

The study results indicate that there are nearly as many mammalian species that have similarly sized males and females as there are species that have larger males. That observation raises the question of why this is the case, Tombak says.

In the 1970s Ralls tried to explain it by putting forward the "big mother" hypothesis, or the idea that larger females might be more capable of producing successful offspring. This still needs to be explored, however.

What can be said for sure, though, is that the new findings will influence "the direction of future research and what kind of questions should be pursued," says Malin Ah-King, an evolutionary biologist at Stockholm University, who was not involved in the research.

"The questioning and reevaluation of prevailing assumptions about sex differences is part of an ongoing process that I call the female turn," she says. "Perceptions about females have [changed] and are still changing away from passive, coy and mating with one male–and now, in mammals, being generally smaller than males."

About the Author

Rachel Nuwer is a science journalist and author. Her latest book is I Feel Love: MDMA and the Quest for Connection in a Fractured World *(Bloomsbury, 2023). Follow her on X @RachelNuwer*

Why Insects Are Lured to Lights in the Night

By Gary Stix & Immy Smith

The enduring image of a moth frantically circling a nocturnal light source—whether candle, campfire or electric bulb—has long intrigued both scientists and literary types, including Shakespeare. ("Thus hath the candle singed the moth," Portia quips in *The Merchant of Venice*.) Entomologists have mulled possible explanations for insects' attraction to all forms of artificial light. The creatures, some have suggested, are drawn to a flame's heat, or they mistake fire or electric light for the moon, which is assumed to act as a kind of celestial compass.

In perhaps the most intensive study to date attempting to answer this question, researchers claim to have come up with "the most plausible model for why insects gather at artificial lights," as reported in *Nature Communications*. Investigators at Imperial College London, Florida International University and the Council on International Educational Exchange discovered through fieldwork and laboratory experiments that insects grow increasingly disoriented around artificial light—so much so that they lose all perspective about which way is up. It turns out that insects ordinarily maintain their up-down orientation by turning their backs toward the sky, the brightest thing they perceive even at night. That allows them to stay properly aligned on a steady flight path.

This evolutionary strategy sufficed for many millions of years, until humans came on the scene with their fire and electricity. When insects encounter an outdoor bulb after dusk, confusion reigns. They tilt their backs toward the bulb as if it were the sky and initiate endless, sometimes erratic loops around it. With light pollution increasing and with drastic declines in insect numbers worldwide, new forms of lighting may be needed to preserve these populations, which are integral to the health of global ecosystems.

With the Sun at Your Back

The tendency of insects to turn their backs toward the light is called the dorsal light response. Bigger animals such as humans can tell up from down based on the pull of gravity sensed directly by the inner ear, among other inputs. Insects' minute sensory organs and their rapid aerial accelerations prevent a moth or a wasp from distinguishing immediately above from below. As a result, they use the sky's brightness as a constant that allows them to self-orient by pointing their backs to the heavens—or at least they did before the arrival of human civilizations that always keep the lights on.

Immy Smith; Source: "Why Flying Insects Gather at Artificial Light," by Samuel T. Fabian et al., in *Nature Communications*, Vol. 15; January 2024 (reference)

Light and Flight Paths

The sustained banking motion that a moth maintains to keep its back to the light results in a relatively unperturbed, orbiting flight path around the lightbulb. At times, though, the moth ends up flying under the bulb and begins a steep upward climb. The insect then begins to stall, losing speed as it climbs before crashing down. Similarly, when the moth flies over the bulb, its inverted orientation at the apex of its flight path can send it plummeting earthward.

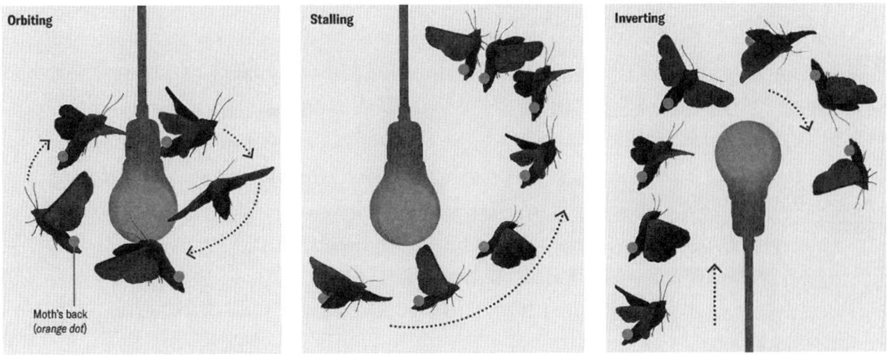

Immy Smith; Source: "Why Flying Insects Gather at Artificial Light," by Samuel T. Fabian et al., in *Nature Communications*, Vol. 15; January 2024 (reference)

Which Way Is Up?

To probe the validity of their back-to-the-light thesis, researchers in the lab at Imperial College London created two opposing scenarios and tested them using high-speed video. In one scenario, ultraviolet light shining from above (simulating the sky) enabled the moths to fly along a stable, linear path. In the other, UV light emitted from the floor caused the insects to tilt, fully invert and come crashing down.

Immy Smith; Source: "Why Flying Insects Gather at Artificial Light," by Samuel T. Fabian et al., in *Nature Communications*, Vol. 15; January 2024 (reference)

About the Author

Gary Stix, senior editor of mind and brain topics at Scientific American, *edits and reports on emerging advances that have propelled brain science to the forefront of the biological sciences. Stix has edited or written cover stories, feature articles and news on diverse topics, ranging from what happens in the brain when a person is immersed in thought to the impact of brain implant technology that alleviates mood disorders such as depression. Before taking over the neuroscience beat, Stix, as* Scientific American's *special projects editor, was responsible for the magazine's annual single-topic special issues, conceiving of and producing issues on Albert Einstein, Charles Darwin, climate change and nanotechnology. One special issue he oversaw on the topic of time in all of its manifestations won a National Magazine Award. With his wife Miriam Lacob, Stix is co-author of a technology primer called* Who Gives a Gigabyte? A Survival Guide for the Technologically Perplexed.

Immy Smith is a UK-based interdisciplinary artist and scientist, focusing on illustration of invertebrates, plants, and lichens.

Do Cats Really Hate Water?

By Meghan Bartels

Cats hate water, but they love fish–and these two stereotypes contradict each other. Although today's furry house rulers can enjoy fishy feasts while staying high and dry, since time immemorial, wild cats have apparently been willing to get their paws wet to snag some tasty treats.

This discrepancy is just one clue that blithely assuming that all cats hate water is a mistake, says Wailani Sung, a veterinary behaviorist at Joybound People & Pets, a rescue and veterinary service in California. "I think when we generalize like that, we do animals a disservice," she says. "Cats are all individuals. Some cats like water. Some cats don't."

In that way, they aren't so different from canines, says Carlo Siracusa, a veterinary behaviorist at the University of Pennsylvania. "We tend to think cats are this unique creature that doesn't like water, but there are many dogs that do not like water," he says.

One key difference between the pet species might have contributed to the stereotype, Sung notes: pet cats tend to stay indoors, whereas dogs are more frequently brought out into the world and taken on adventures, potentially giving them more opportunities to get used to and enjoy being in water. Most pet dogs are also regularly exposed to water through bathing, but cats generally groom themselves with their tongue–no water needed.

Generalizations aside, cats do have some perfectly good reasons to avoid water when possible. Cats have whiskerlike hairs all over their body that help them sense the world around them, and getting these hairs wet might disrupt how they perceive their environment, Sung speculates. Wet fur might also leave a cat vulnerable to the cold, Siracusa says, because cats–like most furry mammals–use their fur to trap air as insulation.

And as prey animals, cats aren't usually fans of unpredictable situations. Despite their fierce hunting skills, cats carry the evolutionary memory of being vulnerable to hungry predators and threatening environments. That means cats are often uncomfortable when their freedom of movement is hampered or when they're put in uncertain and unfamiliar situations. "Cats in general are averse to new stimuli that they feel they cannot control," Siracusa says.

Because healthy cats can groom themselves, there's usually no veterinary reason to worry if your cat can't stand water. "Most cats, if they are not ill, are perfectly able to take care of their coat, and they always look gorgeous," Siracusa says. He encourages owners who want the option of bathing a cat to start slow and let the animal get used to each step in the process while still feeling safe.

House cats, particularly those that are fed dry food, may need to be encouraged to drink water. That's because, over evolutionary time, cats have gotten much of their water from the food they eat rather than needing to find it in the arid home landscapes they evolved in. Siracusa encourages owners to provide multiple water bowls, including at least one that's located away from feeding areas and preferably at a higher elevation in the main living space.

Using a spray bottle of water to punish a cat for misbehavior is a bad idea regardless of how the animal feels about water, both vets agree. Often the response is too delayed for a cat to understand what the incorrect behavior was, leaving them considering their owner unpredictably threatening, Sung says. Instead she recommends confronting bad behaviors more gently. "We definitely want to use positive reinforcement to reinforce the behaviors you do want to see, and you want to distract and redirect when you see something you don't like," Sung says. For example, she says, if your cat jumps on the counter while you're making dinner, perhaps try training them to instead sit on a chair next to you, where they will be praised, petted and comfortable.

And if your cat is one of the many that like water, congratulations! Enjoy the high jinks that likely arise. "Some cats just love water. They sit at the sink, and they meow at the owners until they turn on the faucet," Sung says. "I have certainly had cats that like to play with water in their water bowl, and they splash it everywhere."

About the Author

Meghan Bartels is a science journalist based in New York City. She joined Scientific American *in 2023 and is now a senior news reporter there. Previously, she spent more than four years as a writer and editor at Space.com, as well as nearly a year as a science reporter at* Newsweek, *where she focused on space and Earth science. Her writing has also appeared in* Audubon, Nautilus, Astronomy *and* Smithsonian, *among other publications. She attended Georgetown University and earned a master's degree in journalism at New York University's Science, Health and Environmental Reporting Program.*

'If Not Friend, Why Friend-Shaped?' A Beary Scientific Investigation

By Carin Leong & Allison Parshall

There's a meme about bears floating around the Internet: "If not friend, why friend-shaped?"

This is an intriguing question if you decide to take it seriously. Most deadly apex predators have a certain ferocity to them that doesn't scream "friend"–think lions, wolves and crocodiles. So why do bears seem so cute and cuddly? Have we just been conditioned by teddy bears and Paddington to find them safe and comforting, or is there something else going on? It turns out that evolution and human psychology might help us understand their friend-shaped nature.

"I think that humans have this huge bias in terms of how we see bears," says Rae Wynn-Grant, an ecologist and an affiliated researcher at the University of California, Santa Barbara, who has been studying bears for 14 years. Bears have featured prominently in folklore in many cultures around the world, including some Indigenous cultures in North America that have viewed the animals as humans' kin. We have even seen bears in the sky and named constellations after them. "We have always found ourselves to be quite connected with different species of bears," Wynn-Grant says. "We see ourselves in them."

This deep connection might happen, in part, because humans and the eight known species of bears live in similar environments. People and bears can have a variety of habitats, but both generally thrive in forested areas near bodies of water, such as rivers and lakes. They also have similar dietary habits as omnivores. Fruits, nuts, honey and meat could make a nice dinner for a black bear or a human.

And then there's the physical resemblance–if you squint. "If a human were on all fours, they might resemble a bear. And if a bear was upright, it might resemble a person," Wynn-Grant says. She's not exaggerating: last summer a video of a sun bear in a Chinese zoo went viral because of how uncannily humanlike it looked while standing on its hind legs. (Wynn-Grant fielded many calls from reporters asking her to confirm that it was, indeed, a bear.)

Still, bears have evolved to have plenty of features that we don't, and at least a few of them contribute to their overall friend-shapedness. For one, they have fluffy fur, theoretically perfect for petting. They also have small, rounded ears, which they evolved as an adaptation to conserve heat. Bigger, pointy ears would have more surface area, which would result in the faster transfer of heat.

And then there is bears' big, boopable nose. "When it comes to their sense of smell, that is their superpower," Wynn-Grant explains. "Polar bears can smell their prey under the sea ice from incredibly long distances. So it's their sense of smell that really guides them and is a huge part of their ecology."

Why do we find these features friendly? It could be that we simply think bears look like dogs, which humans domesticated over thousands of years explicitly to be our friends. Tens of millions of years ago, bears and dogs had a common ancestor, and they still share some physical traits. Within the order Carnivora, the two are both part of the suborder Caniformia, which refers to "doglike" carnivores. Other caniforms include racoons, seals, red pandas and otters–which are pretty friend-shaped animals.

Some of bears' features–especially their chubby, rounded face–might also remind us of our own babies. In the 1940s ethologist Konrad Lorenz proposed a so-called baby schema to explain why infants of many species have similar features that are distinct from those of adults: big eyes, a round face and plump cheeks. These sorts of physical traits might trigger a nurturing response in humans, a reaction that helps our offspring survive. Research shows that such traits evoke positive emotions and social connections that can be measured by looking at changes in brain activity and levels of oxytocin, an important bonding hormone.

Bears tend to be very round, plump creatures. So they may appear to be friend-shaped because we have associated those features with harmlessness and social bonding. But the fact that they look like our babies doesn't mean those associations are correct.

"Understand that I am like a bear lover, through and through. [But] I personally don't think that bears look that cuddly. I don't think that they look like friends. When I see bears, I see predators," Wynn-Grant says. For her work, "I sedate them and handle their bodies and do checkups, and I look at their claws and their fangs and stuff. So I'm kind of like, 'Oh, these are vicious animals.'"

The moral of the story: bears may be friend-shaped, but being a good friend to bears doesn't mean taming them or minimizing their wildness. "I think that all wild animals should remain wild and not domesticated, not held in captivity, unless it's for strict conservation reasons," Wynn-Grant says. "Feeling like, 'Oh, bears are just hanging out with us; they're ours,' that actually can move science backward in a direction we don't want."

About the Author

Carin Leong is a documentary filmmaker based in New York. Her projects have received support from Field of Vision, the Singapore International Film Festival, IN-DOCS, and the Tribeca Film Institute. Her work has appeared in Scientific American, Hakai Magazine, *and* The Atlantic. *She holds a master's degree in science journalism from Columbia University's Graduate School of Journalism and is also a graduate of New York University's Tisch School of the Arts.*

Allison Parshall is an associate news editor at Scientific American *who often covers biology, health, technology and physics. She edits the magazine's Contributors column and weekly online Science Quizzes. As a multimedia journalist, Parshall contributes to* Scientific American*'s podcast Science Quickly. Her work includes a three-part miniseries on music-making artificial intelligence. Her work has also appeared in* Quanta Magazine *and* Inverse. *Parshall graduated from New York University's Arthur L. Carter Journalism Institute with a master's degree in science, health and environmental reporting. She has a bachelor's degree in psychology from Georgetown University. Follow Parshall on X (formerly Twitter) @parshallison*

Do Animals Cry When They're Sad?

By Hilde Vervaecke

Last December an Instagram Reel of a "crying" bison—created by photographer Chris Henry—went viral. The video has received more than eight million views and generated thousands of comments. But can bison really be sad? Do nonhuman animals ever cry from sadness?

Tears are useful for our eyes—as they are for many other animals. A lot of mammals, reptiles and birds have tear glands that secrete aqueous fluid. The precise concentrations of biochemical components of tears differ between species and have evolved as adaptations to different environments.

Tears come in three recognized types. Basal tears provide basic maintenance. Glands spontaneously release these tears to deposit a protective nourishing film on the cornea.

Then there are reflex tears, which are produced in response to an external stimulus, such as irritation or injury to the eye. These also spring up after exposure to cold or certain substances, such as the chemicals released by freshly chopped onions. Reflex tears cleanse the eyes and can help heal damage.

The third form consists of emotional tears, which are prompted by one's mental state. Societies have long seen sobs of sadness as a uniquely human behavior—so much so that some communities believed the ability to produce emotional tears could be used as a test of whether someone was secretly a witch or werewolf.

Although its exact function is unknown, there are many hypotheses for why we weep. A good cry may help us cope with challenges by signaling our emotional pain, distress or vulnerability. Our tears can affect the people around us, strengthening social relationships, encouraging cooperative behavior and inhibiting aggression or eliciting care, help or protection.

Today scientific consensus is that emotional tears are indeed uniquely human. But a small amount of evidence hints at some similar occurrences in other animals and has prompted interest from researchers. As one example, even though it is not beneficial for many adult animals to broadcast weakness, many young animals cry without tears to signal their mother. And young deer produce a secretion during stress and hunger from a gland just below the eye to which their mother responds. That same gland is used by adult deer to release scents into the environment.

There are also anecdotes about nonhuman animals that have seemed to be weeping in sadness, including stories of elephants, a sad gorilla and wolves that had become exhausted and fallen behind in the pack. But science has not backed up these stories. For example, in a systematic survey on the subject, published in 1985, people who worked professionally with animals, including veterinarians and zookeepers, reported no observations of an animal crying emotionally.

More recent investigations offer greater nuance. In a study published in 2022, researchers looked at moist or watery eyes in dogs, a phenomenon familiar to anyone who has ever had a puppy. They found that canines secrete tears during a seemingly positive emotional situation: when reuniting with their owner. The hormone oxytocin, which supports bonding, triggers this response. That reaction is something humans notice and appreciate, the study further found. When presented with photographs of dogs, people reported being more eager to care for the pooches with tears in their eyes (something the scientists who took the photographs had produced with saline drops) than for dogs with dryer eyes. Dogs have evolved over the generations to communicate with our species through eye contact. It's possible that they tear up because doing so prompts love and protection from humans; it may even strengthen bonds between us and them.

Researchers have also documented domestic pigs tearing up in poor farm conditions, specifically with increased red staining below the eyes. This fluid is not a true watery tear but rather a secretion of the Harderian gland, something present in many species—though in humans specifically it is poorly developed. In pigs these secretions are also produced by stress. These animals show more staining when they also have lower heart rate variability—another physiological marker of stress—and signs of reduced well-being, such as a bitten-off tail or a display of fear when humans approach. Rats demonstrate the same phenomenon, which is sometimes called "blood tears" because it leaves rust-colored trails in and under the inner corner of the eye. In these rodents, the response increases with environmental stress. It also relates to age and overall well-being–though further study is needed to understand those links.

So what should we make of the "crying bison" video? Though we cannot say that the bison isn't sad, it's more probable that people are anthropomorphizing this unknowing Instagram star–that is, people are attributing human behaviors and characteristics to a nonhuman animal.

Indeed, in a study that presented people with portraits of five different animal species–cats, dogs, horses, chimpanzees and hamsters–people saw images in which tears were added as depicting "sadness," just as it would in humans. In fact, photoshopped tears made these animals seem "less aggressive" and "kinder" to the study participants. People also reported that those animals showed "higher emotional intensity."

We find it extraordinary that a nonhuman animal could be shedding tears in part because we expect that to be a human act–and, in response, we have the urge to respond emotionally to that creature. As to the bull in the video, the Instagram caption suggests he lives free in the wild on the plains of Utah. He appears to be in peak condition and is breathing calmly. He shows no other indication of stress. He stands quietly, watching. It's probable that he had a speck of dust in his eye or the wind had irritated him.

To date, there has been no evidence that suggests bison exhibit emotional crying. That said, more than 20,000 years ago someone painted a bison in the French cave of Chauvet that, some contend, has tears falling from its eyes in a precursor to today's Internet sensation.

This article originally appeared in Eos *and was reproduced with permission.*

About the Author

Hilde Vervaecke is a behavioral biologist at the Odisee University of Applied Sciences in Belgium.

Fact or Fiction?: A Cockroach Can Live without Its Head

By Charles Choi

Cockroaches are infamous for their tenacity, and are often cited as the most likely survivors of a nuclear war. Some even claim that they can live without their heads. It turns out that these armchair exterminators (and their professional brethren) are right. Headless roaches are capable of living for weeks.

To understand why cockroaches–and many other insects–can survive decapitation, it helps to understand why humans cannot, explains physiologist and biochemist Joseph Kunkel at the University of Massachusetts Amherst, who studies cockroach development. First off, decapitation in humans results in blood loss and a drop in blood pressure hampering transport of oxygen and nutrition to vital tissues. "You'd bleed to death," Kunkel notes.

In addition, humans breathe through their mouth or nose and the brain controls that critical function, so breathing would stop. Moreover, the human body cannot eat without the head, ensuring a swift death from starvation should it survive the other ill effects of head loss.

But cockroaches do not have blood pressure the way people do. "They don't have a huge network of blood vessels like that of humans, or tiny capillaries that you need a lot of pressure to flow blood through," Kunkel says. "They have an open circulatory system, which there's much less pressure in."

"After you cut their heads off, very often their necks would seal off just by clotting," he adds. "There's no uncontrolled bleeding."

The hardy vermin breathe through spiracles, or little holes in each body segment. Plus, the roach brain does not control this breathing and blood does not carry oxygen throughout the body. Rather, the spiracles pipe air directly to tissues through a set of tubes called tracheae.

Cockroaches are also poikilotherms, or cold-blooded, meaning they need much less food than humans do. "An insect can survive for weeks on a meal they had one day," Kunkel says. "As long as some predator doesn't eat them, they'll just stay quiet and sit around, unless they get infected by mold or bacteria or a virus. Then they're dead."

Entomologist Christopher Tipping at Delaware Valley College in Doylestown, Pa., has actually decapitated American cockroaches (*Periplaneta americana*) "very carefully under microscopes," he notes. "We sealed the wound with dental wax, to prevent them from drying out. A couple lasted for several weeks in a jar."

Insects have clumps of ganglia–nerve tissue agglomerations–distributed within each body segment capable of performing the basic nervous functions responsible for reflexes, "so without the brain, the body can still function in terms of very simple reactions," Tipping says. "They could stand, react to touch and move."

And it is not just the body that can survive decapitation; the lonely head can thrive, too, waving its antennae back and forth for several hours until it runs out of steam, Kunkel says. If given nutrients and refrigerated, a roach head can last even longer.

Still, in roaches, "the body provides a huge amount of sensory information to the head and the brain cannot function normally when denied these inputs," explains neuroscientist Nick Strausfeld of the University of Arizona, who specializes in arthropod learning, memory and brain evolution. For instance, although cockroaches have a fantastic memory, "when we've tried to teach them when they had bits of them missing, it's hopeless. We have to keep their bodies completely intact."

Cockroach decapitation may seem macabre, but scientists have conducted many experiments with headless roach bodies and bodiless roach heads. Decapitating roaches deprives their bodies of hormones from glands in their heads that control maturation, helping researchers investigate metamorphosis and reproduction. And studies of bodiless roach heads shed light on how their neurons work. Plus, it provides just one more testament to the cockroach's enviable endurance.

Section 2: Myth and Mystery Within Us

How Long Does It Really Take to Form a Habit?

By Jocelyn Solis-Moreira

Waking up at the crack of dawn and going for a run might feel intimidating when you start trying to make it a habit. Weaving a significant new activity such as this into your regular routine obviously takes determination and time—but how much time is really needed to make that habit stick?

One popular idea suggests that it takes 21 days to solidify a habit. A three-week time frame might sound easily reachable to someone making a resolution on New Year's Day, when people tend to feel extra motivated to start a new habit or kick an old one, says Colin Camerer, a behavioral economist at the California Institute of Technology who has conducted research on habit formation. Yet every January 21 very few people can boast that they have kept their resolutions. One survey showed that only 9 percent of people actually stuck to their goals in 2023.

Everyone has a unique habit-building timeline—and no matter how long it is for any individual, repetition is the key to making it work, explains Phillippa Lally, a senior lecturer in psychology and the co-director of the Habit Application and Theory group at the University of Surrey in England. Both Lally and Camerer suggest various individualized ways to reinforce healthy behaviors and to eventually turn a wholesome task into an unconscious habit.

Habit Formation Can Range from a Few Weeks to a Couple of Months

The origin of the "three-week theory" has nothing to do with habits, per se. It apparently originated from the 1960 self-help book *Psycho-Cybernetics*, in which plastic surgeon Maxwell Maltz observed that it took his patients about 21 days to get used to their new appearance after surgery. No formal experiment was conducted to verify this, but the book applied this 21-day timeline to self-transformation in many other wide-ranging aspects of life. For instance, the book also set three weeks as the time needed for people to get used to a new house or change their mind about their beliefs.

Even without much solid research, the 21-day myth became widely accepted. It likely persisted because it seems like such a reasonable amount of time, Camerer explains. Establishing a regular exercise habit in just three days seems too quick and implausible, for example, and a year seems too long and daunting. Camerer says people might easily see 21 days as a realistic and achievable time frame.

Almost a half century later, researchers finally gathered strong evidence that countered this idea. A hallmark 2009 study on habit creation found that habits developed in a range of 18 to 254 days; participants reported taking an average of about 66 days to reliably incorporate one of three new daily activities—eating a piece of fruit with lunch, drinking a bottle of water with lunch or running for 15 minutes before dinner. Consistent daily repetition was the biggest factor influencing whether a behavior would become part of an automatic daily routine, says Lally, who was the first author on the study.

The type of activity is also a factor. Teaching yourself a completely new skill or process obviously takes longer than remembering to drink more water in the morning, Lally notes. A 2015 study found that new gym-goers had to exercise at least four times a week for six weeks in order to develop an exercise habit. And last year Camerer and his colleagues conducted a study that used machine learning to determine the time needed for habit-building. In it, machine-learning models analyzed vast amounts of data on repeated observations of a behavior and factored in different variables that may influence a person's decision to continue the behavior. The results showed that creating a handwashing habit took a few weeks, compared with the half year it took for people to develop an exercise habit. Handwashing, the study noted, is less complex than exercising and offers more opportunities to practice. The researchers also suggested that habit formation depends on the effort that a person puts into practicing an activity and on the presence of environmental cues that would remind them to carry out the behavior.

How to Maintain Consistency When Forming Good Habits

When it comes to keeping a resolution, Camerer notes it can be hard to stay motivated once the initial excitement of a "new year, new me" wears off. This can easily lead to lapsing or even dropping the activity completely after a couple of weeks. Creating a specific plan to perform the activity (for example, "study Spanish grammar for 20 minutes three times a week" versus the vague goal "learn more Spanish") and having some type of accountability (an app tracker or a friend) can help monitor progress and push a person to keep going. Additionally, people are more inclined to keep a resolution that they are interested in doing, rather than one that they simply believe they *should* do.

Rewards are great motivators but only when they're given right away. Lally says that people often make the mistake of delaying gratification–for example, by treating themselves to a shopping trip on Saturday after going to the gym all week. A reward is far more effective if received *during* the task. For instance, a person with an exercise goal could watch a newly released movie while running on the treadmill instead of waiting until the end of the week. Researchers in 2014 had people listen to then popular audiobooks (such as the *Hunger Games* trilogy and *The Devil Wears Prada*) that could only be accessed at the gym during the experiment and found that the participants initially went 51 percent more frequently than the control group.

Another tip Lally recommends is pairing the desired behavior with a reliable cue. For example, if a person goes to the office two days a week, scheduling gym sessions right after work reinforces an association that trains the brain. The more you relate the two behaviors, the stronger the resulting neural connections in brain regions involved in memory and habit formation.

Reconfiguring your physical space may also help. If your goal is to eat more fruit, for instance, Lally says you are more likely to do it if you keep a variety of fruits stocked and on display in your house. This also applies to breaking habits. People partaking in "Dry January" may empty the liquor cabinet beforehand to avoid temptation. While this might help temporarily, drug and alcohol addictions require more serious medical intervention and time.

What Happens if You Miss a Day?

Sometimes life happens; it is completely normal to miss a day or two in any new routine. Lally says that people tend to create rigid schedules that require carrying out a desired behavior every day—even when that's not really feasible. When people cannot meet their own expectations or if the activity itself (such as running 10 miles every day) is too hard, they can be deterred from trying again.

If you feel that you are falling off track, Lally advises taking a beat to evaluate why you are missing days and to come up with ways to fix the problem. Instead of running 10 miles every day, try jogging two miles three times a week. If that's still too challenging, adjust even more by slowing the pace or shortening the distance, and then eventually work yourself back up to the original goal. Putting on sneakers and walking down the block may not seem like much of an achievement at first, but it's a step in the right direction.

So don't kick yourself if you didn't reach your goal by the 21st of this month. As long as you keep at an activity, you *will* get better at it—no matter how long it takes.

About the Author

Jocelyn Solis-Moreira is a freelance journalist covering health and science. She is based in New York State.

Don't Fall for These Five Dangerous Tanning Myths

By Riis Williams

Like exercising and drinking water, protecting yourself from the sun is an important part of primary and preventative health care–regardless of the season. But during summer's longer days, when many people flock outside in pursuit of a golden tan, experts say it's harder to persuade them to take proper safety measures.

Research links unprotected and prolonged sun exposure to several health problems including skin cancer, skin damage and immune system suppression. Yet tanning–whether bathing under natural or artificial ultraviolet (UV) rays–stubbornly remains a hot beauty trend. A survey conducted in March by the Orlando Health Cancer Institute revealed major misconceptions among those eagerly seeking sunshine. Roughly 32 percent of the 1,021 U.S. adult participants said they thought tanning "makes people look better and healthier." And 17 percent reported believing that drinking water helps prevent sunburns.

Such dangerous ideas are likely fueled by Internet trends that promote misinformation about sunscreen and tanning benefits, says Rajesh Nair, an oncology surgeon at the institute, who helped develop the recent survey. "It's almost like there's this battle going on between those who favor a 'natural lifestyle' and push getting that 'natural' glow ... and those who don't," he says. Ahead of the rapidly approaching summer, *Scientific American* spoke with several experts about common tanning and sun exposure myths and ways people can safely enjoy sunshine.

Myth: A "Base Tan" Protects You against Future Sunburns

The so-called base tan may sound like a convenient sunburn protection strategy: hop into a tanning bed or catch some rays outdoors and develop an initial "layer" of tan to prevent future burning during an upcoming sun-filled vacation. But this tactic is not only ineffective; it's also unsafe. Any tan–achieved from either the sun or a tanning bed and "layered" or not–is always a sign of skin damage from UV radiation.

There are two types of UV radiation that affect skin: UVA and UVB. UVA seeps beneath the epidermis, the outermost skin layer, and prompts cells to create a brown pigment called melanin that causes a tan. UVB radiation affects only the epidermis and is responsible for sunburns. Both types of light harm cells, and pretanning before a period of prolonged sun exposure won't stop a person from hurting their skin even further. "If you're just preemptively getting exposure sooner, it does not help you maintain a safer tan or burn less," says Dawn Davis, a dermatologist at the Mayo Clinic.

The only foolproof way a person can protect themself against the sun is to apply sunscreen, wear clothing with plenty of coverage or simply stay out of direct sunlight, Davis says. UV rays can even harm people indoors: sunlight can stream through windows, and some industrial lights emit radiation. "We recommend that people wear a minimum SPF [sun protection factor] 15 when indoors and 30 when outdoors but honestly prefer 30 indoors and 50 outdoors," she says, adding that sunscreen should be reapplied about every two hours. "All individuals should be wearing sunscreen as long as they're over the age of six months. And if you're younger, we suggest shade and clothing."

Myth: Proper Vitamin D Absorption Requires Unprotected Sun Exposure

Vitamin D helps human bodies absorb and process calcium and phosphorus–minerals that support the growth and maintenance of healthy bones. The nutrient can be obtained in two ways: ingestion of vitamin D-rich foods or supplements and absorption of sunlight through the skin.

UVB light triggers skin to produce and retain vitamin D. Clothing and sunscreen do hinder this process because they prevent most UVB rays from interacting directly with the skin. But that doesn't necessarily mean protective measures will lead to vitamin D deficiency, Davis says. In fact, people absorb the nutrient more efficiently by incorporating it into their diet. Davis suggests people rely on fish, fortified milk, fortified breads or vitamin tablets for their daily allowance of vitamin D. Plus, Nair adds, even the strongest sunscreens don't stop all UVB radiation from affecting skin, and people will "still experience penetration of at least 10 percent or so of the sun's rays needed to generate the active form of vitamin D."

Myth: Tanning Helps Treat and Prevent Acne

UV radiation from the sun or a tanning bed can damage inflammatory immune system cells in skin tissue and as a result suppress any existing acne flareups. But the clearer complexion is usually only temporary, Davis says. Tanning or burning regularly can actually worsen acne in the long term by disrupting skin cells' ability to heal scars and blemishes, she says.

Some safer types of light therapy, such as blue light treatments to eliminate skin-residing bacteria that clog pores, can help remedy acne. Davis recommends that people concerned about their complexion speak with a dermatologist about treatment options.

Myth: Tanning Is Risky for Only Older Adults—Not Teens and Young Adults

As people age and their cells reproduce more slowly, skin becomes thinner, wrinkled and more vulnerable to light damage. The immune system's strength generally wanes with time, too, making it especially difficult for older people to recover from sunburns and fight off related infections that can occur when broken or peeled skin is exposed to germs. Older adults should be extra cautious about tanning and prolonged sun exposure–but that doesn't mean teens and young adults are immune to the health repercussions.

Skin cancer, which is typically caused by overexposure to UV radiation, is the most common type of cancer in the U.S., affecting one in five people at some point in their lifetime. It is most commonly diagnosed in older people: in 2018 more than two thirds of new cases of melanoma, the most severe type of skin cancer, were in people age 55 and older. But the disease is currently the fourth most common cancer in people under age 40 in the U.S. (behind breast, thyroid and testicular cancers). And though many types of skin cancer have a high recovery rate when caught early, Nair says that young people are usually less likely to get skin cancer screenings than those age 55 and older, making it especially easy for their diseases to progress unnoticed.

Nair adds that social media users—particularly adolescents and young adults—are constantly exposed to misinformation and disinformation about tanning. Viral Instagram and TikTok posts can induce viewers to ditch sunscreen for unsafe tanning techniques. One such social media trend boasted the use of Pam cooking spray to achieve a golden, toasted-looking glow. This common pantry item is made mostly of canola oil, which does not block UV rays and shouldn't be used in place of sunscreen. Another trend showcases applying sunblock on only parts of the face to generate contrast between tanned and paler skin and exaggerate facial structure—creating a "tanned contour." This leaves uncovered skin vulnerable to the sun; it's much safer to accentuate facial features using makeup.

To steer people away from these types of dangerous fads, public health organizations need to start rethinking how and where they communicate sun safety information, says Jeff Niederdeppe, a communications and public policy professor at Cornell University. "Public health has to meet people where they are—to reach young people on the channels and platforms that they use," he says. "The field recognizes this but may lack the expertise or knowledge about ways that these platforms work and how young people engage with them."

Myth: How Dangerous Tanning Is Depends on a Person's Natural Skin Tone

Although the speed at which an individual tans or burns can vary depending on their natural skin tone, people of all skin shades are susceptible to sun damage; no one is exempt from needing protection. "The healthiest tan is the color of skin that you were born with and that your body makes naturally," Davis says.

As an alternative to suntanning, people looking to achieve a sun-kissed glow should opt for sunless tanning lotions or spray tans, which Davis says contain safe chemicals that won't damage skin cells. Users should, however, be careful to not get these products in their mouth, eyes or nose.

And people shouldn't be terrified of our star, either. "There is absolutely no danger in being active outside in the sunshine," Nair says. "Being outside has tremendous benefits to our psychological and physical health." Both Davis and Nair say that usually the challenge is convincing people they should cap their sun exposure—not get more of it—which is why most doctors push SPF-level products so heavily. In the end, there is no hard rule for the precise amount of time a person can safely spend in the sun. In some cases, especially for people whose jobs require them to be outdoors, risky rays are hard to avoid. The key, Nair says, is to always protect your skin even when you think the sun doesn't look or feel that strong. "Just remember to have all good things in moderation and don't forget plenty of sunscreen," he adds.

About the Author

Riis Williams is a New York City–based science journalist who specializes in climate, health and wildlife reporting. She formerly served as Scientific American's *news intern.*

Do People Really Swallow 8 Spiders a Year While They Sleep?

By Annie Sneed

Rod Crawford has heard plenty of firsthand accounts of spider-swilling slumberers. "Once or twice a year, someone tells me they once recovered a spider leg in their mouth," says Crawford, the arachnid curator at the Burke Museum of Natural History and Culture in Seattle.

Luckily for all of us, the "fact" that people swallow eight spiders in their sleep yearly isn't true. Not even close. The myth flies in the face of both spider and human biology, which makes it highly unlikely that a spider would ever end up in your mouth.

Three or four spider species live in most North American homes, and they all tend to be found either tending their webs or hunting in nonhuman-infested areas. During their forays, they usually don't intentionally crawl into a bed because it offers no prey (unless it has bed bugs, in which case that person has bigger problems). Spiders also have no interest in humans. "Spiders regard us much like they'd regard a big rock," says Bill Shear, a biology professor at Hampden–Sydney College in Virginia and former president of the American Arachnological Society. "We're so large that we're really just part of the landscape,"

More than anything, spiders probably find sleeping humans terrifying. A slumbering person breathes, has a beating heart and perhaps snores—all of which create vibrations that warn spiders of danger. "Vibrations are a big slice of spiders' sensory universe," Crawford explains, "A sleeping person is not something a spider would willingly approach."

From the standpoint of human biology, the oral spider myth also seems ridiculous. If someone is sleeping with her mouth open, she's probably snoring—and thus scaring off any eight-legged transgressors. Plus, many people would likely be awakened by the sensation of a spider crawling over their faces and into their mouths. Shear can attest: once, while camping, he awoke to find a daddy longlegs crawling on his face.

Spider experts concede that a sleeping person could plausibly swallow a spider, but "it would be a strictly random event." People who claim they've swallowed spiders never seem to have any concrete evidence. "People tell me this happened to them, but they threw it (the evidence) away–flushed it down the toilet, usually," Crawford says. There's also a sore lack of eyewitnesses for such a frequent event as eight spiders a year. So even if you heard or read this spider statistic from a trustworthy source (such as a Snapple cap), you can rest assured that it doesn't have a leg, or eight legs, to stand on.

About the Author

Annie Sneed is a science journalist who has written for the New York Times, Wired, Public Radio International *and* Fast Company.

Crack Research: Good News about Knuckle Cracking

By Steve Mirsky

The latest physical anthropology research indicates that the human evolutionary line never went through a knuckle-walking phase. Be that as it may, we definitely entered, and have yet to exit, a knuckle-cracking phase. I would run out of knuckles (including those on my feet) trying to count how many musicians wouldn't dream of playing a simple scale without throwing off a xylophonelike riff on their knuckles first. But despite the popularity of this practice, most known knuckle crackers have probably been told by some expert–whose advice very likely began, "I'm not a doctor, but ..."– that the behavior would lead to arthritis.

One M.D. convincingly put that amateur argument to rest with a study published back in 1998 in the journal *Arthritis & Rheumatism* entitled "Does Knuckle Cracking Lead to Arthritis of the Fingers?" The work of sole author Donald Unger was back in the news in early October when he was honored as the recipient of this year's Ig Nobel Prize in Medicine.

The Igs, for the uninitiated, are presented annually on the eve of the real Nobel Prizes by the organization Improbable Research for "achievements that first make people laugh, and then make them think." In Unger's case, I thought about whether his protocol might be evidence that he is obsessive-compulsive. From his publication: "For 50 years, the author cracked the knuckles of his left hand at least twice a day, leaving those on the right as a control. Thus, the knuckles on the left were cracked at least 36,500 times, while those on the right cracked rarely and spontaneously."

Unger undertook his self and righteous research because, as he wrote, "During the author's childhood, various renowned authorities (his mother, several aunts and, later, his mother-in-law [personal communication]) informed him that cracking his knuckles would lead to arthritis of the fingers." He thus used a half-century "to test the accuracy of this hypothesis," during which he could cleverly tell any unsolicited advice givers that the results weren't in yet.

Finally, after five decades, Unger analyzed his data set: "There was no arthritis in either hand, and no apparent differences between the two hands." He concluded that "there is no apparent relationship between knuckle cracking and the subsequent development of arthritis of the fingers." Evidence for whether the doctor himself was cracked may be that he traveled all the way from his California home to Harvard University to pick up his Ig Nobel Prize in person.

Actually other scholarly studies of the phenomenon had been done. Responding to the Unger paper, Robert Swezey, M.D., wrote to the journal to report that his own 1975 study–co-authored by his then 12-year-old son in an apparent attempt to get the kid's grandma to stop the kvetching over the cracking–also found no crack case for arthritis. Swezey further consulted Rand Corporation statistician John Adams, who noted that "it appears that the [Unger] study was not blinded. Blinding would only be possible if the investigator didn't know left from right. This is not likely since studies indicate that only 31 percent of primary care physicians don't know left from right."

The knuckle kerfuffle reminded me that Stanford University bone development expert David Kingsley got dragged into this field a few years back when his son's fourth grade class asked him if cracking was bad for you. He challenged them to come up with ways to find out while he searched the medical literature. "One kid said that we could divide the room in half," he recalled, "and some of us could really crack our knuckles a lot and the others couldn't, and we could see whether we end up with arthritis–an intervention experiment. I said that this was a great idea. The only problem was that it might take 20 years." Or even 50.

"Then a budding epidemiologist said you could go to old folks homes," Kingsley continued, "and ask everybody if they cracked their knuckles or not and then see whether they had arthritis. And that was exactly the kind of study that I had been able to find." In fact, two such studies did exist, the Swezey work that used 28 nursing home residents and a 1990 paper that examined 300 outpatients. Neither found an increased arthritis incidence among the crackers. So Unger probably could have stopped his study early. Nevertheless, he deserves a big hand.

About the Author

Steve Mirsky was the winner of a Twist contest in 1962, for which he received three crayons and three pieces of construction paper. It remains his most prestigious award.

Your Body Has a Clever Way to Detect How Much Water You Should Drink Every Day

By Claudia Wallis

Serious question: How much water does the average adult need to drink every day? You've probably heard the usual answer: eight 8-ounce glasses, sometimes stated as 8 × 8. But there's not much science behind this ubiquitous recommendation. A 2002 research review found essentially no reliable studies. Any truly serious answer to the how-much question will begin with some version of "it depends." Are you in a hot location? Are you exerting yourself? Are you in good health? How big are you? Do you eat a lot of salty foods, or do you load up on fruits and vegetables?

We do need water every day, but the average person gets it from many sources: tea or coffee, soft drinks (which often include sugar that you don't need), and food. "We typically get about 20 percent of our fluid requirements from solid foods and about 80 percent from beverages," says Brenda M. Davy, professor of human nutrition at Virginia Tech University. Health authorities say that to maintain a healthy balance of water, minerals and salts, adults should drink about a liter (34 ounces) of liquid for every 1,000 kilocalories consumed. That works out to be a little over eight cups for someone who takes in 2,000 daily calories–a possible source of the 8 × 8 notion. But most Americans achieve this level of hydration from a variety of foods and drinks, with about a third coming from plain water, according to a 2013 study of nearly 16,000 U.S. adults.

Natural thirst mechanisms are the reason that most of us do not need to be overly concerned about hydration. The adult body is roughly 60 percent water–closer to 80 percent in the lungs and kidneys–and it carefully controls the concentration of water. We are all familiar with the sensory aspect of this regulation: the dry throat and urgent alert of thirst. But neuroscientists have gained other remarkable insights into how thirst is monitored in the body and controlled in the brain.

Researchers have known since the 1950s that a pea-size structure in the brain's hypothalamus controls thirst. In a series of experiments in which he infused salt into the brains of goats, Swedish physiologist Bengt Andersson showed that a region called the subfornical organ (SFO) monitors the concentration of water and salts in blood and triggers the urge to drink. The SFO plays the same role in people. But Andersson's ideas failed to fully explain how we experience thirst. For instance, when we gulp a drink, we feel almost instantly satisfied, and yet it takes 10 to 15 minutes for a liquid to make it from our mouth, through the digestive tract and into the bloodstream. "Something in the brain is saying that your blood may not have changed conditions yet but that you drank enough water so you can stop feeling thirsty," explains neuroscientist Christopher Zimmerman of Princeton University.

In a series of elegant experiments with mice, Zimmerman and his associates measured the activity of neurons in the SFO. "We saw that their activity changed very fast when the mouse drank water or drank salt water and when it ate food," he says. Their research showed that signals converged on the SFO from several places. "You get a signal from the blood that tells your current state of hydration, a signal from the mouth that tells you how much fluid you drank, and a signal from the gut that tells you what was consumed–was it water, was it something else?" The SFO neurons, he explains, "add these signals together" and then transmit the urge to drink or stop drinking.

The big takeaway of Zimmerman's work is that for the most part you can trust your thirst system to tell you when you need to drink, as opposed to following some arbitrary advice. But there are exceptions. Because the system's sensitivity may decline with age, older adults may need to set reminders to drink–the 2013 study found that, on average, people older than 70 failed to get adequate hydration. People with certain conditions, including kidney stones and diarrhea, also need extra water. And research by Davy and others indicates that middle-aged and older people who are trying to lose weight or maintain weight loss consume fewer calories if they fill up with 16 ounces of water before meals.

Other parts of the brain–the ones used in planning–should help with hydration on hot days and when exercising. Thirsty or not, Zimmerman says, he drinks water before going for a run: "My thirst neurons don't know I'm about to run 10 miles."

About the Author

Claudia Wallis is an award-winning science journalist whose work has appeared in the New York Times, Time, Fortune *and the* New Republic. *She was science editor at* Time *and managing editor of* Scientific American Mind.

Do We Really Use Only 10 Percent of Our Brains?

By Barry L. Beyerstein

Whenever I venture out of the Ivory Tower to deliver public lectures about the brain, by far the most likely question I can expect as the talk winds up is, "Do we really only use 10 percent of our brains?" The look of disappointment that usually follows when I say it isn't so strongly suggests that the 10-percent myth is one of those hopeful shibboleths that refuses to die simply because it would be so darn nice if it were true. I'm sure none of us would turn down a mighty hike in brainpower if it were attainable, and a seemingly never-ending stream of crackpot schemes and devices continues to be advanced by hucksters who trade on the myth. Always on the lookout for a "feel-good" story, the media have also played their part in keeping the myth alive. A study of self-improvement products by a panel of the prestigious National Research Council, *Enhancing Human Performance*, surveyed an assortment of the less far-fetched offerings of the "brain booster" genre and came to the conclusion that (alas!) there is no reliable substitute for practice and hard work when it comes to getting ahead in life. This unwelcome news has done little, however, to dissuade millions who are comforted by the prospect that the shortcut to their unfulfilled dreams lies in the fact that they just haven't quite found the secret to tap this vast, allegedly unused cerebral reservoir.

Why would a neuroscientist immediately doubt that 90 percent of the average brain lies perpetually fallow? First of all, it is obvious that the brain, like all our other organs, has been shaped by natural selection. Brain tissue is metabolically expensive both to grow and to run, and it strains credulity to think that evolution would have permitted squandering of resources on a scale necessary to build and maintain such a massively underutilized organ. Moreover, doubts are fueled by ample evidence from clinical neurology. Losing far less than 90 percent of the brain to accident or disease has catastrophic consequences. What is more, observing the effects of head injury reveals that there does not seem to be any area of the brain that can be destroyed by strokes, head trauma, or other manner, without leaving the patient with some kind of functional deficit. Likewise, electrical stimulation of points in the brain during neurosurgery has failed so far to uncover any dormant areas where no percept, emotion or movement is elicited by applying these tiny currents (this can be done with conscious patients under local anesthetic because the brain itself has no pain receptors).

The past hundred years has seen the advent of increasingly sophisticated technologies for listening in on the functional traffic of the brain. The goal of behavioral neuroscience has been to record electrical, chemical and magnetic changes in brain activity and to correlate them with specific mental and behavioral phenomena. With the aid of instruments such as EEGs, magnetoencephalographs, PET scanners and functional MRI machines, researchers have succeeded in localizing a vast number of psychological functions to specific centers and systems in the brain. With nonhuman animals, and occasionally with human patients undergoing neurological treatment, recording probes can even be inserted into the brain itself. Despite this detailed reconnaissance, no quiet areas awaiting new assignments have emerged.

All told, the foregoing suggests that there is no cerebral spare tire waiting to be mounted in service of one's grade point average, job advancement, or the pursuit of a cure for cancer or the Great American Novel. So, if the 10-percent myth is that implausible, how did it arise? My attempts to track down the origins of the 10-percent myth have not discovered any smoking guns, but some tantalizing clues have emerged (more are recounted in the references below). One stream leads back to the pioneering American psychologist, William James, in the late 19th and early 20th centuries. In addition to his voluminous scholarly work, James was a prodigious author of popular articles offering advice to the general public. In these exhortatory works James was fond of stating that the average person rarely achieves but a small portion of his or her potential. I was never able to find an exact percentage mentioned, and James always talked in terms of one's undeveloped potential, apparently never relating this to a specific amount of gray matter engaged. A generation of "positive thinking" gurus that followed were not so careful, however, and gradually "10 percent of our capacity" morphed into "10 percent of our brain." Undoubtedly, the biggest boost for the self-help entrepreneurs came when the famous adventurer and journalist Lowell Thomas attributed the 10-percent-of-the-brain claim to William James. Thomas did so in the preface he wrote, in 1936, to one of the best-selling self-help books of all time, Dale Carnegie's *How to Win Friends and Influence People*. The myth has never lost its steam since.

Other sources for the ubiquity of the 10-percent myth probably come from popular authors' misconstrual of scientific papers by early brain researchers. For example, in calling (for technical reasons) a huge percentage of the cerebral hemispheres the "silent cortex," early investigators may have left the mistaken impression that what is now referred to as the "association cortex" had no function. That was far from the researchers' intention, but that is what seems to have filtered through to the public. Likewise, early researchers' appropriately modest admissions that they didn't know what 90 percent of the brain was doing probably fostered the widespread misconception that the leftovers did nothing.

In my quest for the seminal utterance of the 10-percent myth, I frequently came across the claim that Albert Einstein had once explained his own brilliance by reference to the myth–Einstein's enormous prestige, of course, making it unassailable thenceforth. A careful search by the helpful people at the Albert Einstein archives, however, was unable to provide me with any record of such a statement on his part. So it remains probably just another of those instances where promoters with a point or a buck to make have misappropriated the clout of Einstein's name to further their own endeavors.

The 10-percent myth has undoubtedly motivated many people to strive for greater creativity and productivity in their lives–hardly a bad thing. The comfort, encouragement and hope that it has engendered helps explain its longevity. But, like so many uplifting myths that are too good to be true, the truth of the matter seems to be its least important aspect.

The Adult Brain Does Grow New Neurons After All, Study Says

By Karen Weintraub

If the memory center of the human brain can grow new cells, it might help people recover from depression and post-traumatic stress disorder (PTSD), delay the onset of Alzheimer's, deepen our understanding of epilepsy and offer new insights into memory and learning. If not, well then, it's just one other way people are different from rodents and birds.

For decades, scientists have debated whether the birth of new neurons–called neurogenesis–was possible in an area of the brain that is responsible for learning, memory and mood regulation. A growing body of research suggested they could, but then a Nature paper last year raised doubts.

Now, a new study published in March in another of the Nature family of journals–*Nature Medicine*–tips the balance back toward "yes." In light of the new study, "I would say that there is an overwhelming case for the neurogenesis throughout life in humans," Jonas Frisén, a professor at the Karolinska Institute in Sweden, said in an e-mail. Frisén, who was not involved in the new research, wrote a News and Views about the study in the March issue of *Nature Medicine*.

Not everyone was convinced. Arturo Alvarez-Buylla was the senior author on last year's Nature paper, which questioned the existence of neurogenesis. Alvarez-Buylla, a professor of neurological surgery at the University of California, San Francisco, says he still doubts that new neurons develop in the brain's hippocampus after toddlerhood.

"I don't think this at all settles things out," he says. "I've been studying adult neurogenesis all my life. I wish I could find a place [in humans] where it does happen convincingly."

For decades, some researchers have thought that the brain circuits of primates–including humans–would be too disrupted by the growth of substantial numbers of new neurons. Alvarez-Buylla says he thinks the scientific debate over the existence of neurogenesis should continue. "Basic knowledge is fundamental. Just knowing whether adult neurons get replaced is a fascinating basic problem," he says.

New technologies that can locate cells in the living brain and measure the cells' individual activity, none of which were used in the *Nature Medicine* study, may eventually put to rest any lingering questions.

A number of researchers praised the new study as thoughtful and carefully conducted. It's a "technical tour de force," and addresses the concerns raised by last year's paper, says Michael Bonaguidi, an assistant professor at the University of Southern California Keck School of Medicine.

The researchers, from Spain, tested a variety of methods of preserving brain tissue from 58 newly deceased people. They found that different methods of preservation led to different conclusions about whether new neurons could develop in the adult and aging brain.

Brain tissue has to be preserved within a few hours after death, and specific chemicals used to preserve the tissue, or the proteins that identify newly developing cells will be destroyed, said María Llorens-Martín, the paper's senior author. Other researchers have missed the presence of these cells, because their brain tissue was not as precisely preserved, says Llorens-Martín, a neuroscientist at the Autonomous University of Madrid in Spain.

Jenny Hsieh, a professor at the University of Texas San Antonio who was not involved in the new research, said the study provides a lesson for all scientists who rely on the generosity of brain donations. "If and when we go and look at something in human postmortem, we have to be very cautious about these technical issues."

Llorens-Martín said she began carefully collecting and preserving brain samples in 2010, when she realized that many brains stored in brain banks were not adequately preserved for this kind of research. In their study, she and her colleagues examined the brains of people who died with their memories intact, and those who died at different stages of Alzheimer's disease. She found that the brains of people with Alzheimer's showed few if any signs of new neurons in the hippocampus–with less signal the further along the people were in the course of the disease. This suggests that the loss of new neurons–if it could be detected in the living brain–would be an early indicator of the onset of Alzheimer's, and that promoting new neuronal growth could delay or prevent the disease that now affects more than 5.5 million Americans.

Rusty Gage, president of the Salk Institute for Biological Studies and a neuroscientist and professor there, says he was impressed by the researchers' attention to detail. "Methodologically, it sets the bar for future studies," says Gage, who was not involved in the new research but was the senior author in 1998 of a paper that found the first evidence for neurogenesis. Gage says this new study addresses the concerns raised by Alvarez-Buylla's research. "From my view, this puts to rest that one blip that occurred," he says. "This paper in a very nice way... systematically evaluates all the issues that we all feel are very important."

Neurogenesis in the hippocampus matters, Gage says, because evidence in animals shows that it is essential for pattern separation, "allowing an animal to distinguish between two events that are closely associated with each other." In people, Gage says, the inability to distinguish between two similar events could explain why patients with PTSD keep reliving the same experiences, even though their circumstances have changed. Also, many deficits seen in the early stages of cognitive decline are similar to those seen in animals whose neurogenesis has been halted, he says.

In healthy animals, neurogenesis promotes resilience in stressful situations, Gage says. Mood disorders, including depression, have also been linked to neurogenesis.

Hsieh says her research on epilepsy has found that newborn neurons get miswired, disrupting brain circuits and causing seizures and potential memory loss. In rodents with epilepsy, if researchers prevent the abnormal growth of new neurons, they prevent seizures, Hsieh says, giving her hope that something similar could someday help human patients. Epilepsy increases someone's risk of Alzheimer's as well as depression and anxiety, she says. "So, it's all connected somehow. We believe that the new neurons play a vital role connecting all of these pieces," Hsieh says.

In mice and rats, researchers can stimulate the growth of new neurons by getting the rodents to exercise more or by providing them with environments that are more cognitively or socially stimulating, Llorens-Martín says. "This could not be applied to advanced stages of Alzheimer's disease. But if we could act at earlier stages where mobility is not yet compromised," she says, "who knows, maybe we could slow down or prevent some of the loss of plasticity [in the brain]."

About the Author

Karen Weintraub is a staff writer at USA Today, *where she covers COVID, vaccine development and other health issues.*

Fact or Fiction?: If You Shave (or Wax), Your Hair Will Come Back Thicker

By Dina Fine Maron

We scrunch. We twist. We pull the skin on our faces or legs taut just so razors can whisk away the undesired hairs sprouting on the fertile landscape of our bodies. Yet many of us do these tasks with a sense of futility, of inevitable failure, because we believe this regular ritual of removal causes hair to grow back mightier than before—rising like a phoenix renewed but with even coarser, thicker or darker offerings.

That is simply not so. But there are several reasons that the myth continues to flourish. One is the limitation of human perception. "People are just not very good observers, but there's just no science behind hair growing back thicker," says Amy McMichael, chair of the Department of Dermatology at Wake Forest Baptist Health. There's also the power of coincidence. Indeed, pervasive myths—if a young boy shaves his mustache it will grow back thicker—are grounded in a kernel of truth: it might. But that's because the shaving may overlap with the timing of natural hormonal fluctuations in his body that are developing his adult facial hair, not because of his hair removal. Body hair grows at different times and at different rates for everybody.

The very act of cutting may make hair appear thicker for a short time. A human hair shaft is like a pencil or javelin that tapers at the end. So when a razor slices away the tip, it may appear that the remaining hair, and subsequent stubble, is thicker or darker than it was before the cut. Those short hairs, sticking straight up from their follicles, may even appear coarser. But cutting away part of the hair does not typically change anything about that regrowth process. The tapered hair you had is the hair you'll get back. (Although, in rare instances, excessive waxing, which tears a hair from its root, can eventually reduce growth from certain hair follicles due to the repeated trauma).

The medical literature has actually tackled this abiding hair question with studies directly comparing the hair regrowth among shavers versus au naturel growth for some 100 years. In 1928, for example, four men agreed to be part of a hair regrowth study attempting to settle the matter. The men shaved a portion of their faces in one downward stroke using the same brand of shaving soap, fresh razors and water at a constant temperature–all in the name of science. The study authors collected the shorn hairs and compared 100 of them after each measuring, arriving at their chief conclusion: There is no evidence that shaving accelerates the rate of beard growth.

In a somewhat more recent study five healthy young white men agreed to explore how repeated shaving impacts human hair regrowth. Each volunteer shaved one leg weekly for several months while leaving the other leg as a control (likely opting to wear long pants during the study period). The study, published in 1970, found no significant differences in the hair width, coarseness or rate of growth. That type of data jives with what dermatologists see in their practices, says Melanie Grossman, a dermatologist based in New York City. "Women shave their legs all the time. They would be like gorillas if the hair was coming back thicker or darker," McMichael agrees. "Plus we would never have to think about hair loss on our heads if cutting the hair shaft would make it come back thicker."

With hair waxing the story is similar. Hair is not coming back in a more robust way after it's yanked out by the roots. Still, there are other genetic or hormonal influences that can affect hair growth. And environment can play a role, too. "If you scratch an area of your skin significantly (which doesn't happen with an average shaving or waxing), it may get rough like a callus and that can actually stimulate thickening of the hair growth. That's because the skin is getting thicker, the nerves are getting thicker and the hair may get thicker, too. But that is not typical," McMichael says.

There's also another factor to think about as a hair springs up through the skin for the first time—at first it may appear ever-so-slightly darker since it has not yet been lightened by exposure to pollutants, chemicals and the sun. But that minute impact will not last. So let's try to put this myth to rest—although, like our hair, it will likely reemerge.

About the Author

Dina Fine Maron, formerly an associate editor at Scientific American, *is now a wildlife trade investigative reporter at* National Geographic.

Section 3: Weather Myths: Separating Fact from Fiction

Fact or Fiction?: South of the Equator Toilets Flush and Tornadoes Spin in the Opposite Direction

By Robynne Boyd

Weather isn't always predictable. If it were, daily forecasts would be spot-on, hurricanes anticipated, and picnics safe from abrupt summer downpours. Instead, climate systems are complex, and tornadoes are no exception. So, whereas guessing the direction of a tornado's torque is possible, like any weather prediction the forecast will only be correct most of the time.

It's true that tornadoes tend to revolve counterclockwise in the Northern Hemisphere and clockwise in the Southern Hemisphere. However, according to research meteorologist Richard Rotunno of the U.S. National Center for Atmospheric Research in Boulder, Colo., the opposite has also occurred. There has even been the occasional appearance of both counterclockwise and clockwise rotating tornadoes under the same thunderstorm. These deviations undercut the common misperception that the direction of a tornadoes' spin results from the Coriolis force.

To set the record straight, Rotunno explains that the Coriolis force only has a significant influence on the spin direction of Earth's largest atmospheric and oceanographic circulation systems, such as the Gulf Stream, jet stream, trade winds and hurricanes. Earth's rotation around its axis causes this effect, making Northern Hemisphere winds deflect to the right and those in the Southern Hemisphere deflect to the left. It is also why an airplane flying from Anchorage to Miami must consider the Earth's counterclockwise rotation (as seen from the North Pole) to land at its destination, instead of splashing into the Gulf of Mexico.

The Coriolis force isn't, however, omnipotent, compelling all currents great and small to spin counterclockwise when north of the equator and clockwise to its south. Though many people have seen videos of toilets flushing in Australia and the U.S. that swirl in opposite directions, these experiments are based on luck and, perhaps not surprisingly, the toilets' varying designs. Pranksters have even gone so far as to blame the Coriolis effect for hair curling in a certain direction.

Despite the large amount of misinformation, toilets–and even tornadoes–are too small to be affected by the Coriolis, whose force would only begin to directly influence a storm's swirling mass if it were approximately three times larger than the supercell storm systems that typically generate tornadoes.

"Tornadoes are only indirectly influenced by the Coriolis force," says meteorologist Harold Brooks of the National Oceanic & Atmospheric Administration's National Severe Storms Laboratory in Norman, Okla. The majority of tornadoes happen in "tornado alley," in the Great Plains of the U.S., but they can happen anywhere in the world, including southern Brazil, northeastern Argentina and Bangladesh. These violently roiling columns of air originate from parent thunderstorms called supercells. In the U.S., supercells form when dry polar air from Canada meets moist tropical air from the Gulf of Mexico, causing the warm air to rapidly rise.

The upwelling current of air within a thunderstorm is referred to as an updraft. "If sufficient vertical wind shear (the increase of wind speed with height) exists, this updraft will rotate," Brooks says. "Tornadoes usually rotate in the same direction as the thunderstorm they're associated with." Therefore, if the warm winds blowing north from the equator meet cool upper-level winds out of the west, the tornado will rotate counterclockwise. And if the warm equatorial winds blow to the south and clash with aloft winds, a tornado will rotate clockwise.

This is because in both hemispheres, upper-level winds blow out of the west due to planetary rotation. These winds are Coriolis's subtle claim to a tornado's torque.

Although understanding Coriolis's weak influence over the direction of a tornado's spin seems feasible, fully grasping how tornadoes function may not be. And predicting exactly when and where tornadoes will occur—and which way they will spin—seems even less so. Uncertainty may be the only certainty of weather.

About the Author

Robynne Boyd began writing about people and the planet when living barefoot and by campfire on the North Shore of Kauai, Hawaii. Over a decade later and now fully dependent on electricity, she continues this work as an editor for IISD Reporting Services. When not in search of misplaced commas and terser prose, Robynne writes about environment and energy. She lives in Atlanta, Georgia.

Mysterious Gamma-Ray Flashes May Be Missing Link for Lightning Bolts

By Lee Billings

It's said that lightning never strikes the same place twice and a watched pot never boils.

But neither statement is true—especially when your "pot" is an enormous tropical lightning storm bristling with thunderbolts and you're watching it from far above in the stratosphere. Two recent studies in *Nature* found that some storms are indeed at a rolling boil—one that emits powerful bursts of gamma rays, not steam. And some of these emissions occur in mysterious, previously unrecognized patterns, split-second flickers that seem to spark ordinary lightning discharges.

"How lightning gets started inside thunderstorms is a big mystery," says Joseph Dwyer, a physicist at the University of New Hampshire, who served as a reviewer for both studies. "Decades of balloon and aircraft measurements have failed to find electric fields inside storms large enough to make a spark, and yet thunderstorms manage to make more than eight million flashes per day around the planet. We are clearly missing something important. These new observations could be that 'something.'"

Scientists have long known that thunderstorms can produce gamma rays, extremely high-energy light that is more often associated with astrophysical phenomena, such as exploding stars and matter-devouring black holes. In earthly tempests, the physics behind such emissions is relatively well-understood: swirling, windblown water droplets and ice crystals build up an electric charge within a storm, with positively charged particles rising to the cloud tops and negatively charged ones sinking to the bottom. This results in a sprawling electric field on the order of 100 million volts—powerful enough to accelerate electrons inside the storm to nearly the speed of light, slamming the charged particles into air molecules that give off further electrons and setting off a cascade of collisions so energetic that gamma rays are ultimately produced.

Researchers had observed two forms of thunderstorm gamma-ray emissions: relatively long-lived "glows" lasting hundreds of seconds, as well as intense, microsecond-scale bursts known as terrestrial gamma-ray flashes (TGFs), bright enough to be visible to Earth-observing satellites.

But scientists also knew this picture was incomplete, built as it was on piecemeal readings from airborne and ground-based instruments. "We still have significant uncertainties in the electrical nature of storms, from the details of how charge is separated by particles within the cloud to the physics of lightning initiation and channel development," says Vanna Chmielewski, an atmospheric scientist at the National Oceanic and Atmospheric Administration's National Severe Storms Laboratory, who was not involved in the new research. "Many of these processes are difficult if not impossible to accurately capture in a laboratory setting or model, given the number of contributing factors, known variability within even a single storm and limited observational datasets which can be used for validation."

To get a clearer view, in 2023 a team led by Nikolai Østgaard and Martino Marisaldi, both atmospheric physicists at the University of Bergen in Norway, monitored the gamma-ray emissions of large storms from up close and on high, chasing down thunderheads with 10 flights of a NASA-owned modified U-2 spy plane over the Caribbean and Central America. The program, called ALOFT (Airborne Lightning Observatory for Fly's Eye Geostationary Lightning Mapper Simulator and Terrestrial Gamma-Ray Flashes), constitutes the most comprehensive and focused airborne surveillance of thunderstorm gamma-ray emissions yet performed.

"ALOFT was designed to try to definitively answer the question 'Are these gamma-ray flashes and glows common or rare?'" says Steve Cummer, an electrical engineer at Duke University and co-author of both studies. "And it delivered big time.... The gamma-ray production process is way, way more important than we thought."

The flights revealed glows and TGFs, as expected, but also much more: Both phenomena proved far more abundant than predicted, with most of the TGFs being dim enough to escape the notice of any overwatching satellites. The glows also weren't steadily emanating from isolated regions in the storms as anticipated but rather bubbled up in surges of radiation for hours across regions about 100 kilometers wide. And amid the hundreds of recorded events, the researchers also glimpsed something new—so-called flickering gamma-ray flashes (FGFs), pulsing spikes of emission that lasted for milliseconds and seemed to spring from glows. Most intriguingly, Østgaard says, "all the transient gamma-ray events were followed by intense lightning."

The dynamism and large volume of these high-energy events, the researchers say, hint that the electron avalanches at their source act to limit a thunderstorm's large-scale electric fields, in addition to spurring lightning production. "Thunderstorms are generating so much ionizing radiation that they partially discharge themselves in some regions, causing the electric fields to shoot up in other regions within the storm," Dwyer says. "These field enhancements could be large enough to initiate lightning."

Altogether, Marisaldi says, the ALOFT results paint a new, more nuanced picture that demands follow-up studies. "The acceleration of charged particles to relativistic energies within thunderclouds, for which gamma rays are a proxy, is an intrinsic and very common process, at least in convective tropical clouds," he says. "Our observations suggest an intriguing hypothesis: a glowing thundercloud might be a prerequisite for lightning initiation. The glow can evolve locally in unstable phenomena—such as FGFs and TGFs—leading to the inception of lightning. We are eager to test this hypothesis with another flight campaign."

Future flights, he says, could examine the emissions of storms at higher latitudes, as well as investigate two other major tropical hot spots for lightning, located in Central Africa and Southeast Asia.

About the Author

Lee Billings is a science journalist specializing in astronomy, physics, planetary science, and spaceflight, and is a senior editor at Scientific American. *He is the author of a critically acclaimed book,* Five Billion Years of Solitude: the Search for Life Among the Stars, *which in 2014 won a Science Communication Award from the American Institute of Physics. In addition to his work for* Scientific American, *Billings's writing has appeared in the* New York Times, *the* Wall Street Journal, *the* Boston Globe, Wired, New Scientist, Popular Science, *and many other publications. Billings joined* Scientific American *in 2014, and previously worked as a staff editor at* SEED *magazine. He holds a B.A. in journalism from the University of Minnesota.*

Fact or Fiction?: If the Sky Is Green, Run for Cover—A Tornado Is Coming

By Meredith Knight

If the sky turns green during a thunderstorm, gather up your pets and other loved ones and head for the cellar, a twister is on the way. So goes the common wisdom in much of the central U.S.—and other tornado-prone regions in the world, like Australia—when faced with a threatening sky (although some swear green means hail). Scientifically speaking, however, little evidence supports either the tornado or hail claims, though there is some evidence for green thunderstorms.

Over the past 15 years, a small group of scientists have weathered the elements working on green thunderstorms as a pet project, publishing a handful of articles in meteorological journals. All point to the existence of green skies with severe thunderstorms but no direct connection to tornadoes or hail can be made.

"Green skies are associated with severe weather," says physicist and occasional green thunderstorm guru Craig Bohren at Pennsylvania State University. "In areas where tornados are common, they are said to be the cause of green storms. Or you will be told, often with considerable vehemence, that hail causes the greenness. Both explanations are easily refuted by observations."

The first question researchers faced: Is a green sky real, or just an optical illusion caused by light reflected off the ground and back up into the sky, as some green sky dissenters suggest? Frank Gallagher, now a meteorologist for the U.S. Army at Dugway Proving Ground in Utah, tackled this issue for his thesis at the University of Oklahoma. He joined a tornado-chasing research team called VORTEX and recorded the wavelengths of light coming from storms in Texas and Oklahoma using a spectrophotometer, a tool about the size of an old video camera that can measure the color and intensity of light.

Gallagher found that the dominant wavelength of light was green in several severe thunderstorms and that the color was independent of the terrain underneath the storm. As meteorology professor William Beasley, Gallagher's advisor at Okalahoma, put it, "[He] measured green wavelengths of light over a green wheat field and over freshly plowed fields with red-brown Oklahoma dirt."

Threatening green skies during a thunderstorm also proved entirely independent of the type of severe weather that came with it. Gallagher measured hailstorms where the dominant wavelength of light was green as well as hailstorms where it was the typical gray-blue color of thunderstorms. Tornado-producing storms proved similarly divorced from any particular sky color, other than dark.

Researchers remain undecided about the exact mechanisms that cause the sky to appear green in certain thunderstorms, but most point to the liquid water content in the air. The moisture particles are so small that they can bend the light and alter its appearance to the observer. These water droplets absorb red light, making the scattered light appear blue. If this blue scattered light is set against an environment heavy in red light–during sunset for instance–and a dark gray thunderstorm cloud, the net effect can make the sky appear faintly green. In fact, green thunderstorms are most commonly reported in the late afternoon and evening, according to Beasley.

In a paper published in the *Journal of Applied Meteorology*, Gallagher also suggested that green thunderstorms might occur more frequently than thought. Because it gets quite dark during thunderstorms, the purity of light may be too poor for observers to see the color on most occasions.

Other research on green thunderstorms is limited and not well funded. As Penn State's Bohren says, this is "not exactly a hot topic of research. Indeed, being curious about them can be hazardous to one's career." For example, his small grant from the National Science Foundation for the portable spectrophotometer Gallagher used was derided by then Speaker of the House Newt Gingrich's office and Richard Pombo, then a Republican congressman from

California, who denounced Bohren in the *Congressional Record*. (Of course, neither politician hailed from "tornado alley.")

Joshua Wurman at the Center for Severe Weather Research in Boulder, Colo., agrees: "I wouldn't call [the green sky] one of the burning issues in tornado science." Nevertheless, the research that is out there suggests that the green colored sky some might observe during a severe thunderstorm does have limited predictive power for those who live in areas where severe weather occurs, like Dorothy–and her little dog, too.

About the Author

Meredith Knight is a freelance science and health writer based in Austin, Texas.

Section 4: It's Science!

The Myth of Stephen Hawking

By Charles Seife

There was almost a religious reverence in the hush that descended upon the audience at the beginning of a Stephen Hawking lecture. Typically, every seat was taken, and if the fire marshals weren't a force to be reckoned with, there were large clots of people near the exits and in the aisles, craning their necks to get their first view of the physicist. And as he wheeled out onto stage, the audience was palpably awed. "Sometimes there were 30 or 40 seconds of pure silence," says Christophe Galfard, one of Hawking's graduate students who himself became a popularizer of science. "For me, it was the silence that made it so ... that's what triggered my wish to pursue that road."

But despite Hawking's passion for sharing his work in cosmology and astrophysics with the public, few in the audience were there to learn about his science. They were there to be in the presence a person who had ascended Mount Sinai and been granted a glimpse of the secrets of the cosmos. Hawking was a great scientist, but in his quest for recognition, he took on the mantle of a prophet. It was a Faustian bargain that made Hawking the preeminent scientist of our lifetimes–but at a cost.

When a prophet speaks, he speaks with all the confidence and infallibility of divine revelation. Yet a scientist's trade, the very fabric of his profession, is uncertainty. Almost by definition, a biologist or a physicist or a chemist has a head filled with inaccurate information; even those with the biggest egos realize that much of the knowledge they've built up over the years is tentative, incomplete or even outright wrong. Indeed, the scientist's whole purpose is to reduce that uncertainty by just a little bit. While prophets are always right, good scientists, trained to strive to be a little less wrong, are by nature tentative and conditional. And this makes them easy to ignore even when they're the only kind of authorities that count.

Not Stephen Hawking. Once he assumed the mantle of a prophet in the late 1980s, Stephen Hawking would never be ignored. His books were all but guaranteed to sell, whether or not they were well written or even comprehensible. His lectures were typically sold out, with hopefuls packing the aisles to try and get a better look at the famous physicist. He could command an audience like no other scientist; the press and the public would hang on his every word–even when those words didn't have anything to do with his work on black holes or cosmology, or even betray any deep insight or knowledge.

Hawking managed to convince the public that his opinion always mattered. "[H]is comments attracted exaggerated attention even on topics where he had no special expertise," wrote Martin Rees, a close friend and colleague of his, "for instance philosophy, or the dangers from aliens or from intelligent machines." His overweening confidence–and his stubbornness–cost him respect from many of his colleagues, especially late in his career.

Perhaps the most difficult aspect of Hawking's transformation into a celebrity, however, was entangled with his disability. Just as he began to make himself known on the physics circuit, his disease (amyotrophic lateral sclerosis, also known as Lou Gehrig's disease) began to bite. Hawking always suspected that his quick rise through the physics ranks, his early awards, his appointment to the Royal Society at the tender age of 32–even his appointment to the Lucasian chair that Isaac Newton held several centuries before him–all resulted from his disability rather than his physics prowess. "I think I was appointed as a stopgap to fill the chair as someone whose work would not disgrace the standards expected of the Lucasian chair, but I think they thought I wouldn't live very long, and then they could choose again, by which time they could find a more suitable candidate," he once told an interviewer. "Well, I'm sorry to disappoint the electors."

As much as this doubt nagged at Hawking throughout his life–he truly wanted to be recognized for his science rather than for his perserverance in the face of disability–Hawking realized that his celebrity, if not his physics, was founded on the latter as much as the former. It disturbed him that his outsized reputation was due to the caricature of him a disabled genius–that he was viewed as a seer gifted with extraordinary insight in compensation for a bodily incapacity. But at the same time, he embraced it and even helped build the myth to increase his renown.

The cost to Hawking was that the myth obscured the humanity of the person behind it. In truth, Hawking was not the greatest scientist of our time. He was an important physicist whose importance is almost universally misunderstood; a person who suffered deeply and also caused deep suffering; a celebrity scientist who broke the mold of his forebears and fundamentally changed the concept of a scientific celebrity. To truly understand Hawking–just as to truly understand science–one has to reject the myth and examine the messy reality underneath. To stop looking at Hawking as a prophet, but instead as a flawed and brilliant human being.

About the Author

Charles Seife is director of the Arthur L. Carter Institute of Journalism at New York University and the author of seven books, including a history of fusion, Sun in a Bottle, *and a biography of a major scientist,* Hawking Hawking.

Fact or Fiction?: Mammoths Can Be Brought Back from Extinction

By David Biello

In a petri dish in the bowels of Harvard Medical School scientists have tweaked three genes from the cells of an Asian elephant that help control the production of hemoglobin, the protein in blood that carries oxygen. Their goal is to make these genes more like those of an animal that last walked the planet thousands of years ago: the woolly mammoth.

"Asian elephants are closer to mammoths than either is to African elephants, yet quite different in appearance and temperature range," notes Harvard geneticist and technology developer George Church. "We are not trying to make an exact copy of a mammoth, but rather a cold-resistant elephant."

But what if the new–and fast advancing–techniques of genome editing allowed scientists to engineer not only cold-resistance traits but also other characteristics of the woolly mammoth into its living Asiatic relatives? Scientists have found mammoth cells preserved in permafrost. If they were to recover cells with intact DNA, they could theoretically "edit" an Asian elephant's genome to match the woolly mammoth's. A single cell contains the complete genetic instruction set for its species, and by replicating that via editing a new individual can, theoretically, be created. But would such a hybrid–scion of an Asian elephant mother and genetic tinkerers–count as a true woolly mammoth?

In other words, is de-extinction a real possibility?

The answer is yes. On January 6, 2000, a falling tree killed the last bucardo, a wild Iberian ibex, which is a goatlike animal. Her name was Celia. On July 30, 2003, Celia's clone was born. To make the clone scientists removed the nucleus of a cell from Celia intact and inserted it into the unfertilized egg cell of another kind of ibex. They then transferred the resulting embryo to the womb of a living goat. Nearly a year later they delivered the clone by cutting her from her mother.

Although she lived for a scant seven minutes due to lung defects, Celia's clone proved that not only is de-extinction real, "it has already happened," in the words of environmentalist Stewart Brand, whose San Francisco-based Long Now Foundation is funding some of this de-extinction research, including Church's effort as well as bids to bring back the passenger pigeon and heath hen, among other candidate species. Nor is the bucardo alone in the annals of de-extinction. Several viruses have already been brought back, including the flu variant responsible for the 1918 pandemic that killed more than 20 million people worldwide.

And yet, the bucardo remains extinct. The lack of progress stems partly from a lack of funds, according to Alberto Fernández-Arias, the Spanish wildlife veterinarian who helped lead the bucardo cloning effort. But it also has to do with flaws in the method used to bring the species back to life. Researchers in Asia have been using the technique for a decade or more to try to resurrect the mammoth—to no avail.

New genome editing techniques—in particular the CRISPR system Church and his team are using—offer new hope, however. In 1987 Japanese scientists found genetic sequences dubbed "clustered regularly interspaced short palindromic repeats" in *Escherichia coli* bacteria. These CRISPRs, as they are known, were subsequently found to be ubiquitous in many bacteria, where they defend against viruses—a simple but effective immune system.

Specifically, the enzyme known as Cas9 (for CRISPR-associated system 9) can attach itself to specific DNA in a virus and cut it, following the lead of an RNA guide. That cut kills the pathogen or at least disables it. And now geneticists, armed with the right RNA sequence to guide Cas9 exactly where they want it to go (an outcome still not always guaranteed), can unleash this editor from the *Streptococcus pyogenes* bacteria to add or subtract code from many genes, such as those that produce hemoglobin in the Asian elephant genome or even genes in human cells. Moreover, with the right RNA guide CRISPR can edit up to five genes at once—a number that keeps growing as scientists continue to experiment. And RNA is quick and cheap to make with machines.

Combined with Church's own technique—a combination of robotics and genetic experimentation known as "multiplex automated genome engineering," or MAGE—the entire five billon or so base pairs of the Asian elephant genome can be broken down into their constituent parts and then reassembled in the image of a mammoth's genetic code. As it stands, Church and his team have tinkered with three genes and hope to test their viability in organs soon. "We need to construct and characterize Asian elephant stem cells and organs derived from these [stem cells]," he says.

This new technique is not confined to just resurrecting extinct species. Yeast, tobacco, rice, wheat, rats, rabbits, frogs and fruit flies are just a few of the 20 or so organisms to have their genes altered this way to date. The tinkering could prove profound: Church has suggested that the genes that protect certain extremophile bacteria against the harmful effects of radiation could be added to the human genome to enable long-distance space travel, to take one far-out example.

Such genome editing could also be used to add much needed genetic diversity back into species with precariously small populations, such as the cheetah or Sumatran rhino. By taking DNA from dead individuals and incorporating it into the genomes of survivors, what were gene puddles might be restored to gene pools.

Such species play critical roles in their home ranges, helping shape entire forests or savannas. And that's the hope for a resurrected bucardo or woolly mammoth as well. The mammoth steppe of Siberia might be brought back one day, along with the great herds of woolly proboscideans. The woolly Asian elephant hybrids Church envisions might even help stave off the new global warming human society is presently engineering by sequestering CO_2 in a restored Siberian steppe, according to Russian geophysicist Sergey Zimov, who has lead efforts to create such a Pleistocene Park in northeastern Siberia. Of course, introduction of any species, even one that used to live in a particular place, could prove difficult because it would have to coexist with plants, humans and other animals that have adapted to living in an area without the introduced species.

Ultimately, given the primary focus of genetic advances like CRISPR, the easiest species to resurrect would not be the recently vanished passenger pigeon or the mammoth–it would be the Neandertal. There appear to be just slightly more than 30,000 genetic mutations that differentiate us from them–and *Homo sapiens* is the complicated organism best understood by human geneticists.

But resurrecting an extinct hominid opens a new dimension to the ethical concerns around this scientific potential. "Neandertals were sentient human beings," wrote evolutionary geneticist Svante Pääbo of the Max Planck Institute for Evolutionary Anthropology in Germany in a recent *New York Times* op–ed. "In a civilized society we would never create a human being in order to satisfy scientific curiosity," he observed. Pääbo and his colleagues were the first to sequence the Neandertal genome.

Such de-extinction–whether of Neandertal or mammoth–may never come to pass, but the technologies that make it possible could help prevent extinction in the first place by restoring genetic vigor to imperiled species. And with human activities currently fueling a new mass extinction, perhaps it is good that de-extinction continues to edge further away from fiction and closer to fact. Or, as Church notes of the fact of de-extinction: "I'm skeptical that there will be a clean defining moment."

About the Author

David Biello is a contributing editor at Scientific American.

The Idea That a Scientific Theory Can Be 'Falsified' Is a Myth

By Mano Singham

J.B.S. Haldane, one of the founders of modern evolutionary biology theory, was reportedly asked what it would take for him to lose faith in the theory of evolution and is said to have replied, "Fossil rabbits in the Precambrian." Since the so-called "Cambrian explosion" of 500 million years ago marks the earliest appearance in the fossil record of complex animals, finding mammal fossils that predate them would falsify the theory.

But would it really?

The Haldane story, though apocryphal, is one of many in the scientific folklore that suggest that falsification is the defining characteristic of science. As expressed by astrophysicist Mario Livio in his book *Brilliant Blunders*: "[E]ver since the seminal work of philosopher of science Karl Popper, for a scientific theory to be worthy of its name, it has to be falsifiable by experiments or observations. This requirement has become the foundation of the 'scientific method.'"

But the field known as science studies (comprising the history, philosophy and sociology of science) has shown that falsification cannot work even in principle. This is because an experimental result is not a simple fact obtained directly from nature. Identifying and dating Haldane's bone involves using many other theories from diverse fields, including physics, chemistry and geology. Similarly, a theoretical prediction is never the product of a single theory but also requires using many other theories. When a "theoretical" prediction disagrees with "experimental" data, what this tells us is that that there is a disagreement between two sets of theories, so we cannot say that any particular theory is falsified.

Fortunately, falsification–or any other philosophy of science–is not necessary for the actual practice of science. The physicist Paul Dirac was right when he said, "Philosophy will never lead to important discoveries. It is just a way of talking about discoveries which have already been made." Actual scientific history reveals that scientists break all the rules all the time, including falsification. As philosopher of science Thomas Kuhn noted, Newton's laws were retained despite the fact that they were contradicted for decades by the motions of the perihelion of Mercury and the perigee of the moon. It is the single-minded focus on finding what works that gives science its strength, not any philosophy. Albert Einstein said that scientists are not, and should not be, driven by any single perspective but should be willing to go wherever experiment dictates and *adopt whatever works*.

Unfortunately, some scientists have disparaged the entire field of science studies, claiming that it was undermining public confidence in science by denying that scientific theories were objectively true. This is a mistake since science studies play vital roles in two areas. The first is that it gives scientists a much richer understanding of their discipline. As Einstein said: "So many people today–and even professional scientists–seem to me like somebody who has seen thousands of trees but has never seen a forest. A knowledge of the historic and philosophical background gives that kind of independence from prejudices of his generation from which most scientists are suffering. This independence created by philosophical insight is–in my opinion–the mark of distinction between a mere artisan or specialist and a real seeker after truth." The actual story of how science evolves results in inspiring more confidence in science, not less.

The second is that this knowledge equips people to better argue against antiscience forces that use the same strategy over and over again, whether it is about the dangers of tobacco, climate change, vaccinations or evolution. Their goal is to exploit the slivers of doubt and discrepant results that always exist in science in order to challenge the consensus views of scientific experts. They fund and report their own results that go counter to the scientific consensus in this or that narrow area and then argue that they have falsified the consensus. In their book *Merchants of Doubt*, historians Naomi

Oreskes and Erik M. Conway say that for these groups "[t]he goal was to fight science with science–or at least with the gaps and uncertainties in existing science, and with scientific research that could be used to deflect attention from the main event."

Science studies provide supporters of science with better arguments to combat these critics, by showing that the strength of scientific conclusions arises because credible experts use comprehensive bodies of evidence to arrive at consensus judgments about whether a theory should be retained or rejected in favor of a new one. These consensus judgments are what have enabled the astounding levels of success that have revolutionized our lives for the better. It is the *preponderance of evidence* that is relevant in making such judgments, not one or even a few results.

So, when anti-vaxxers or anti-evolutionists or climate change deniers point to this or that result to argue that they have falsified the scientific consensus, they are making a meaningless statement. What they need to do is produce a preponderance of evidence in support of *their* case, and they have not done so.

Falsification is appealing because it tells a simple and optimistic story of scientific progress, that by steadily eliminating false theories we can eventually arrive at true ones. As Sherlock Holmes put it, "When you have eliminated the impossible, whatever remains, however improbable, must be the truth." Such simple but incorrect narratives abound in science folklore and textbooks. Richard Feynman in his book *QED*, right after "explaining" how the theory of quantum electrodynamics came about, said, "What I have just outlined is what I call a 'physicist's history of physics,' which is never correct. What I am telling you is a sort of conventionalized myth-story that the physicists tell to their students, and those students tell to their students, and is not necessarily related to the actual historical development which I do not really know!"

But if you propagate a "myth-story" enough times and it gets passed on from generation to generation, it can congeal into a fact, and falsification is one such myth-story.

It is time we abandoned it.

About the Author

Mano Singham is a Fellow of the American Physical Society and the retired director of the University Center for Innovation in Teaching and Education and adjunct associate professor of Physics at Case Western Reserve University. His latest book is The Great Paradox of Science: Why its conclusions can be relied upon even though they cannot be proven *(Oxford University Press).*

Why Does the Moon Look Bigger Near the Horizon?

By Phil Plait

I remember watching the full moon rise one early evening a while back. I first noticed a glow to the east lighting up the flat horizon in the darkening sky, and within moments the moon was cresting above it. It looked huge! It also seemed so close that I could reach out and touch it. I gawped at it for a moment and then smiled. I knew what I was actually seeing: the moon illusion.

Anyone who has seen the moon (or the sun) near the horizon has experienced this effect. The moon looks enormous there, far larger than it does when it's overhead. I'm an astronomer, and I know the moon is no bigger on the horizon than at its zenith, yet I can't *not* see it that way. It's an overwhelming effect. But it's not real. Simple measurements of the moon show it's essentially the same size on the horizon as when it's overhead. This really is an illusion.

It's been around a while, too: the illusion is shown in cuneiform on a clay tablet from the Assyrian city Nineveh that has been dated to the seventh century B.C.E. Attempts to explain it are as old as the illusion itself, and most come up short. Aristotle wrote about it, for example, attributing it to the effects of mist.

This isn't correct; the illusion manifests even in perfectly clear weather. A related idea, still common today, is that Earth's air acts like a lens, refracting (bending) the light from the moon and magnifying it. But we know that's not right, because the moon is measurably the same size no matter where it is in the sky. Examining the physics of that explanation shows that it falls short as well. In fact, although the air near the horizon does indeed act like a lens, its actual effect is to make the sun and moon look squished, like flat ovals, not to simply magnify them. So that can't be the cause, either.

Another common but mistaken explanation is that when the moon is on the horizon, you subconsciously compare it with nearby objects such as trees and buildings, which make it look bigger. But that can't be right, because the illusion still occurs when the horizon is empty, such as at sea or on the plains. Also, if you're in a city and see the moon high in the sky between buildings, it appears to be its normal size, so this can't be the explanation.

Yet the moon *does* look bigger on the horizon. Experiments in the 1950s and 1960s by cognitive psychologists Irvin Rock and the late Lloyd Kaufman showed that people perceive the moon as much larger on the horizon—sometimes as much as three times bigger than when it's overhead. If the visual cues to the position of the moon go away, however, the illusion vanishes. Looking at it through a paper towel tube, for example, makes it look the same size no matter where in the sky it is.

So what's the cause? Like with so many things in science, two effects are at play. One is the Ponzo illusion (not to be confused with a Ponzi scheme, an investment illusion). It's a very simple yet overwhelming illusion. In its simplest forms, two parallel horizontal lines of equal length (like an equal sign) are placed between two lines that are nearly vertical but converge slightly near the top. When you look at the horizontal lines, the top one appears longer even though they're the same length. It's almost impossible not to see them as unequal.

Variations abound, but all rely on tricking the brain by using perspective. We interpret the two nearly vertical lines not as leaning toward each other but as parallel yet converging in the distance, like railroad tracks. This effect, in which lines in two-dimensional space appear to meet at a point called the vanishing point, is often used in art to portray relative distances.

The key is that the two horizontal lines are the same length. Our brain sees that, but it also perceives the top line as farther away. If it's farther away and the same apparent size, according to our brain's messed-up logic, it must be physically larger than the lower line, so it appears bigger. This is very similar to the wonderful Ames room illusion, in which distorted walls and angles make two people of equal height appear to have wildly different sizes depending on where in the room they stand.

The Ponzo illusion is the heart of the moon illusion, but there's more to it. If I were to ask you what shape the sky over your head appears to be, you'd probably say it's a hemisphere—a half of a sphere. But we don't actually perceive it that way. If we did, you'd see the zenith, the point directly over your head, as the same distance from you as any point on the horizon. Yet experiment after experiment shows that's not the case: we see the horizon as farther away and the sky as more like a flat-bottomed bowl overhead, with the zenith closer to us.

That's not too surprising, actually. If you're outside on a cloudy day, the clouds over your head really *are* closer to you; they might be five kilometers above you, but the ones near the horizon can be more than 100 kilometers distant. So we've evolved to think of the sky as flattened that way.

Now put the two together: When the moon is on the horizon, we think it's farther away. But the moon's size in the sky isn't actually changing, so our brain interprets this as the moon looking huge. When it gets higher in the sky, we perceive it as being closer, so it winds up looking smaller.

Amazingly, this explanation, at least in part, was determined around 1,000 years ago. The brilliant medieval philosopher Ibn al-Haytham studied vision and optics and made major contributions to both. He examined the moon illusion and correctly noted that an object of fixed size will look smaller if it's perceived as closer and will look bigger if it's farther away. He thought intervening objects such as trees or buildings made the moon appear closer and therefore bigger, which we now know isn't correct. But he had the basic idea down, and he came closer than many who lived much later.

Misconceptions about the moon illusion still abound, and like so many myths, they probably won't go away no matter how much people like me write about them. But in this case, we do know the right explanation, and it's one of the paradoxes of science: we know why this illusion occurs, but it stubbornly persists.

About the Author

Phil Plait is a professional astronomer and science communicator in Virginia. His column for Scientific American, *The Universe, covers all things space. He writes the* Bad Astronomy Newsletter. *Follow him online.*

Section 5: Food Fallacies: Myths We Believe

To Follow the Real Early Human Diet, Eat Everything

By Kate Wong

Paul Saladino is stripped to the waist, biceps bulging as he works a butcher's saw back and forth across a cow femur. When he finally severs the bone, a crowd of onlookers erupts in cheers. Flashing a smile, he checks to make sure he's being filmed, then scoops a spoonful of marrow from the center of one piece of bone. He then deposits it in the mouth of an eager young woman like a priest giving communion.

Saladino, a medical doctor, is a popular proponent of an animal-based diet that exalts meat and organs and demonizes vegetables. Through videos like this one on TikTok, as well as the podcast he hosts, he preaches the value of eating beef and liver, marrow and testicles to millions of followers on social media. He is the author of the 2020 book *The Carnivore Code* and a companion cookbook. He founded the company Heart and Soil, which sells organ-based supplements, and co-founded Lineage Provisions, which sells protein powder and meat sticks. Saladino contends that the traditional food pyramid, with its broad base of plant foods that narrows into animal foods, is upside down and that the medical establishment's view that high cholesterol causes heart disease is wrong. He says that meat and organs are the key to health, strength and vitality.

Saladino is not alone in his carnivorous pursuits. TikTok, Instagram and YouTube are teeming with influencers peddling meat-centric menus. Like the so-called paleo or caveman diets before them, these diets shun ultraprocessed foods such as potato chips, breakfast cereals, packaged breads, sodas and hot dogs. But they are significantly more restrictive than the paleo diet where plant foods are concerned. Some advocates, Saladino and celebrity adventurer Bear Grylls among them, allow for a limited amount of fruit but discourage vegetables, which they contend are loaded with defensive chemicals that are toxic to humans. Others, such as Canadian psychologist Jordan Peterson and his podcast host daughter, Mikhaila, champion a diet of beef, salt and water alone. Many, like social media personality Brian Johnson, aka Liver King, recommend consuming animal products–including dairy and eggs–raw.

Meatfluencers, as they are known, often characterize their regimens as "ancestral," made up of the foods our ancient predecessors ate. If this is what our ancestors ate, they argue, then this is what the human body is supposed to consume. "If you align your diet and lifestyle with millions of years of human and hominid evolution," Saladino says in another TikTok appearance, "that is how humans thrive."

Studies of the remains of our forebears, as well as observations of living primates and modern-day hunter-gatherers, refute the idea that humans evolved to subsist primarily on animals. Meat did play a significant role in our evolution. Yet that doesn't mean we're meant to eat like lions. Real ancestral human diets are difficult to reconstruct precisely, but they were vastly more varied than the mostly meat diets of carnivores, a finding that has important implications for what people today should eat to be healthy.

To be fair to the promoters of flesh-forward diets, scientists have traditionally paid a lot of attention to meat eating in human evolution, as have journalists who write about our origins (including me). Several factors have contributed to this trend. For one thing, we humans are unique among primates in regularly hunting animals that are as large as or larger than ourselves, and scientists are particularly interested in understanding traits that set us apart from other creatures. For another, stone tools and butchered animal bones are more readily preserved in the archaeological record than fragile plant remains. And then there's the fact that the hunting of animals–particularly large, dangerous mammals such as elephants–is inherently more exciting than the quiet business of gathering berries, nuts and tubers. In any case, it doesn't take a lot of googling to turn up a heap of scientific papers and popular articles touting the idea that hunting and eating meat made us human.

Interest in the role of meat and hunting in human origins has deep roots. Charles Darwin even speculated about its importance in his 1871 treatise, *The Descent of Man*, and *Selection in Relation to Sex*. Ideas about how carnivory shaped human evolution have shifted over the years, but the prevailing wisdom is this: around two million years ago *Homo erectus*, an early member of our genus, began evolving modern human body proportions, with longer legs, shorter arms, a smaller gut and a larger brain. The earliest stone tools and animal bones bearing cut marks date to before that period. The timing suggests that the invention of sharp-edged stone tools allowed early humans to butcher large animals and have access to a rich new source of calories. This nutritious food required less processing in the gastrointestinal tract, which allowed our energetically expensive gut tissue to shrink. Calorie-dense meat also provided fuel that allowed our energetically expensive brains to expand. A feedback loop took hold: as brains ballooned, our increasingly clever ancestors dreamed up ever more effective tools for procuring energy-rich animal foods, fueling more brain growth in Homo.

If that were all we knew about human evolution, it'd be tempting to conclude that we evolved to eat a meat-based diet. But that's only a piece of what anthropologists and archaeologists have learned about food and human origins, and even that chapter of our story has undergone revision over the past 15 years in light of new evidence. Fresh fossil discoveries and novel DNA analyses are revealing what our ancestors ate in unprecedented detail. For a clearer understanding of the evolution of humans and our diet, we need to take a closer look at what happened before and after that two-million-year mark.

Let's start at the beginning. Humans, monkeys and apes make up a subset of primates known as the higher primates, which evolved to eat fruit. The hominin lineage (*Homo sapiens* and its extinct relatives, including *Ardipithecus*, *Australopithecus*, and others) dates to roughly six million to seven million years ago. Fossils of the earliest known hominins indicate that they walked upright on two legs but still spent a lot of time in trees. They don't appear to have made stone tools and probably subsisted on a diet similar to that of chimpanzees and bonobos, our closest living relatives–which is to say mostly fruits, nuts, seeds, roots, flowers and leaves, along with insects and the occasional small mammal.

For the entire first half of our known history, hominins seem to have maintained this plant-based diet–they left no material trace of meat eating. It's not until nearly three million years after our lineage got its start that there's any evidence that they exploited large animals for food.

The oldest possible evidence of meat eating by hominins comes from Dikika, Ethiopia. There researchers found fragments of bone from goat- and cow-size mammals bearing marks suggestive of butchery that occurred at least 3.39 million years ago. The butcher, in this case, was probably *Australopithecus afarensis*, the small-brained, small-bodied hominin species to which the famous Lucy fossil belongs–the only hominin species known from this time and place. Although no tools were discovered, based on the pattern of damage to the bones, the researchers concluded that *A. afarensis* used sharp-edged stones to strip flesh from the bones and struck the bones with blunt stones to access the marrow inside.

The oldest stone tools come from the site of Lomekwi in northwest Kenya. Like the cut-marked bones from Dikika, these 3.3-million-year-old implements significantly predate the origin of our genus, *Homo*, and seem instead to be the handiwork of the small-brained australopiths. Both occurrences also appear to be isolated in time, a flash in the evolutionary pan, separated by the next oldest evidence for stone tools and butchery by hundreds of thousands of years.

It's only after two million years ago that hominins started to incorporate large game into their diet more routinely, according to Briana Pobiner, a paleoanthropologist at the Smithsonian National Museum of Natural History, who studies the evolution of meat eating in humans. The site of Kanjera South in southwestern Kenya, which records hominin activities from around two million years ago, is one of the earliest sites to preserve evidence of what researchers call persistent carnivory. There early members of *Homo* transported choice rocks from as many as 10 kilometers away to make their stone tools. They used these tools to extract meat and marrow from a variety of mammals that lived in the surrounding grasslands, from small antelopes to bovids the size of wildebeests. Some of the antelopes appear to have been acquired intact, presumably through hunting. The larger animals may have been scavenged. However they procured the carcasses, the Kanjera hominins butchered animals at this site repeatedly, over generations, the bones spanning a sediment layer three meters thick.

The hominins at Kanjera went back to this place again and again to butcher animals, but their pattern of persistent carnivory was not widespread elsewhere. Nor was it followed by a steady increase in meat eating over time, as would be expected in the feedback-loop scenario. W. Andrew Barr of George Washington University and his colleagues, including Pobiner, analyzed the evidence for hominin meat consumption in the zooarchaeological record of eastern Africa from between 2.6 million and 1.2 million years ago. Although the evidence for meat eating increases shortly after two million years ago with the debut of *H. erectus*, the first hominin to attain modern body proportions, the study found that this pattern is the result of a sampling bias: researchers have simply collected more archaeological material from this time period than from earlier intervals. Their findings, Barr, Pobiner and their co-authors concluded, did not support the hypothesis that meat made us human.

"When I think about changes in diet over time, I don't think the change was linear," Pobiner says. In many ways, the changes have been more about broadening the diet rather than progressing from vegetarian to meat eater, she explains. "Humans are omnivores," she says. "We've always been omnivores."

Even at Kanjera, with its impressive accumulation of butchered bones, meat wasn't the only food on offer. Analyses of the cutting edges of a sample of stone tools from the site revealed that most of the implements exhibit wear patterns characteristic of tools that have been used in experiments to chop herbaceous plants and their underground storage organs—those tubers, bulbs, roots and rhizomes that plants produce to store carbohydrates. A smaller proportion showed signs of animal-tissue processing.

As much as the evolution of meat eating is a focus of her work, Pobiner says, "that doesn't mean that I think that it was ever the most significant component of early human diets."

It's possible that early humans were targeting fat rather than meat when they first started butchering animals. Jessica Thompson of Yale University and her colleagues argue that before hominins invented stone tools suitable for hunting large animals, they may have used simpler implements to scavenge abandoned carcasses for their nutritious marrow and brains. Lean meat such as that from wild animals is energetically expensive to metabolize, and in the absence of fat in the diet, it can cause protein poisoning and other ills. Smashing scavenged bones to get to the marrow could have produced the extra nutrients needed to fuel brain growth before our ancestors developed the more complex technology needed for hunting.

The fat and meat of terrestrial mammals weren't the only possible source of extra calories for hungry hominins. Fish, shellfish, and other aquatic animals and plants sustained our forebears who lived near rivers, lakes and oceans. As early as 1.95 million years ago, *Homo* was exploiting fish and turtles, among other aquatic foods, in Kenya's Turkana Basin.

Our ancestors may have also wrung more calories from plant and animal foods by cooking them. Richard Wrangham of Harvard University has proposed that cooking, which makes food easier to chew and digest, may have provided *Homo* with the extra fuel needed to power a bigger brain. In 2022 researchers announced that they had found remains of fish that may have been cooked with controlled heat 780,000 years ago at the site of Gesher Benot Ya'aqov in Israel.

There is another place where scientists can look for clues to what early humans ate: their teeth. When researchers analyzed the tartar preserved in the stained teeth of two *Australopithecus sediba* individuals from South Africa, they found microscopic bits of silica from plants these hominins ate nearly two million years ago, including bark, leaves, sedges and grasses.

Even the Neandertals, our burly cousins who ruled Eurasia for hundreds of thousands of years and are known for having been skilled big-game hunters, consumed plants. Amanda Henry of Leiden University in the Netherlands and her colleagues found traces of legumes, dates and wild barley in the tartar on their fossilized teeth. And researchers led by Karen Hardy of the University of Glasgow discovered roasted starch granules in Neandertal teeth, indicating that they ate cooked vegetables. Some Neandertals might have even forgone animal flesh entirely: in a study co-led by Laura Weyrich of Pennsylvania State University, analyses of DNA preserved in the tartar of Neandertals found in El Sidrón cave in Spain turned up traces of pine nuts, moss and mushrooms–and no meat whatsoever.

Researchers have developed other techniques for studying what hominins put in their mouths and chewed, such as measuring the chemical isotopes in teeth, but these methods have important limitations: they can't determine the proportion of animal versus plant foods in the diet. To that end, another tartar study offers an inkling. James Fellows Yates of the Max Planck Institute for Evolutionary Anthropology in Leipzig, Germany, and his colleagues analyzed DNA from bacteria preserved in Neandertal tartar and compared it with bacterial DNA from the teeth of modern chimps, gorillas, howler monkeys and modern humans. The team found that the Neandertals and modern humans in its sample had a group of *Streptococcus* bacteria in their mouths that the nonhuman primates didn't have. These strep bacteria eat sugars from starchy foods, such as roots, seeds and tubers. Their presence in the mouths of the Neandertals and modern humans–but not the nonhuman primates, which eat mostly nonstarchy plant parts–indicates that *Homo* had adapted to eating an abundance of starchy plant foods by the time Neandertals and modern humans split from their last common ancestor around 600,000 years ago. This timing hints that a high-carb diet helped to power brain expansion in *Homo*.

Other features of teeth suggest additional leads in the quest to understand what our ancestors ate. If you look at hominin tooth morphology over time, says paleoanthropologist and evolutionary biologist Peter Ungar of the University of Arkansas, you see that australopiths had big, flat teeth with thick enamel–traits that indicate they were specialized for crushing hard foods such as seeds. *Homo*, for its part, evolved smaller teeth with crests that were better suited to eating tough foods, including meat. Yet we obviously lack the long, sharp canine teeth that carnivores have for stabbing and tearing at prey and the sharp-edged carnassial teeth for shearing flesh.

"We're not pure carnivores, we never were," Ungar says. "Our teeth are not designed for meat eating." That doesn't mean we can't survive on animal tissue, he notes–cutting and cooking both make meat easier for us to consume–but "anybody who's chewed on beef jerky long enough knows that our teeth really aren't designed for that. Or, for that matter, raw steak."

The microscopic pits and scratches that foods leave on the teeth reinforce this message. Whereas *Australopithecus* microwear patterns reflect a narrow range of food types, early *Homo* shows a somewhat wider range. Later members of our genus show microwear texture patterns that indicate they ate even more kinds of foods. Although these lines of evidence are limited, Ungar says, they suggest *Homo* became a more versatile eater, capable of consuming a wider variety of foods than its predecessors. This versatility would have served our ancestors well as they spread into new environments with a greater diversity of food types on offer.

Proponents of animal-based diets are fond of pointing to the Hadza, a group of foragers in northern Tanzania, to make their case for going hard on meat. Saladino and Liver King name-check them regularly in their social media videos. "I can tell you very clearly that the Hadza don't give a shit about vegetables. They don't really eat vegetables," says Saladino, who once visited the Hadza on an excursion set up for tourists.

Anthropologists who have lived with the Hadza and studied their diet for years would disagree. Herman Pontzer of Duke University notes that for decades researchers have observed that plant foods make up at least 50 percent of the Hadza diet. The Hadza are not unique in this regard. Hunter-gatherers around the world get roughly half their calories from plant foods and half from animal foods on average. But that average obscures the real value of the hunting-and-gathering strategy, which is that it allows people to subsist on a wide variety of diets depending on what's available in their environment at a given time of year. Long-term studies of the Hadza show that some months they may get most of their calories from honey; other months they may eat mostly plant foods, including root vegetables. There are times they hardly eat any meat at all.

What made humans so triumphant wasn't that we swapped out plants for animals but that we added hunting to our repertoire. Hunting and gathering reliably produces more calories a day than any other primate strategy, Pontzer says. The reason it works is that it's a mixed portfolio. "You have some people going after high-value, hard-to-get animals with a lot of protein and fat, which is great," he says. "And you have people who are going after more dependable plant foods. It's the balance of those things that makes it so successful."

Hunting and gathering produces so many calories, in fact, that people can afford to share them with other group members, including children, whose brains take longer to develop than in other species and who need more time to learn how to fend for themselves. A strict plant eater can't do that, because although the number of calories one can get every day eating plants is very dependable, it might not be high enough to produce a surfeit of calories. A strict meat eater, on the other hand, will have long periods of famine between feasts that do not, on average, generate extra calories. But when we put those two things together, Pontzer observes, we generate a surplus. And that surplus, he surmises, is the variable that's made energetically expensive human things such as large brains and extended childhood possible.

What the fossil, archaeological and ethnographic evidence indicates, then, is that there is no one diet that nature prescribed for us. What our ancestors ate varied dramatically over time and space, driven in no small part by what was available to them as seasons changed, climate shifted, and populations spread into new ecosystems. Forged in that crucible of uncertainty, we evolved the ability to survive and thrive on an impressive diversity of foods. Hunter-gatherers around the world eat diets with wildly different proportions of plant and animal foods, and all of them appear to be healthy, protected from heart disease, diabetes, and other maladies that are common in industrial populations.

So what is a person looking to eat healthily supposed to do? "I think what it says is you should feel liberated to try a bunch of different diets and find one that works for you," Pontzer says. But "when somebody tells you that there's only one way to eat, they are wrong, and you can stop listening."

About the Author

Kate Wong is an award-winning science writer and senior editor at Scientific American *focused on evolution, ecology, anthropology, archaeology, paleontology and animal behavior. She is fascinated by human origins, which she has covered for more than 25 years. Recently she has become obsessed with birds. Her reporting has taken her to caves in France and Croatia that Neandertals once called home, to the shores of Kenya's Lake Turkana in search of the oldest stone tools in the world, to Madagascar on an expedition to unearth ancient mammals and dinosaurs, to the icy waters of Antarctica, where humpback whales feast on krill, and on a "Big Day" race around the state of Connecticut to find as many bird species as possible in 24 hours. Kate is co-author, with Donald Johanson, of* Lucy's Legacy: The Quest for Human Origins. *She holds a bachelor of science degree in biological anthropology and zoology from the University of Michigan. Follow Wong on X (formerly Twitter) @katewong*

Fact or Fiction?: The 5-Second Rule for Dropped Food

By Larry Greenemeier

You're about to savor your first bite from a delicious candy apple when, just as your teeth are about to sink in, the fruit–candy combo slips from its stick and plummets to the ground. The clock is ticking. You quickly snatch the fallen morsel, well within five seconds—the acknowledged time limit for determining whether dropped food should end up in your mouth or in the trash.

What happens next is generally a judgment call depending on several factors—what was dropped, where it was dropped and the victim's level of hunger. What to do could also pivot on whether or not the most recent health column you read covering this topic on the Web said that you could get away with putting the dropped food in your mouth without a trip to the emergency room. A lot of research—and common sense, really—might indicate that any dropped food carries a risk of collecting bacteria. So the only real questions might be how great the risk is and whether it's worth taking.

Food retrieved just a few seconds after being dropped is less likely to contain bacteria than if it is left for longer periods of time, researchers at Aston University's School of Life and Health Sciences in England recently reported. The Aston team also noted that the type of surface on which the food has been dropped has an effect, with bacteria least likely to transfer from carpeted surfaces. Bacteria is much more likely to linger if moist foods make contact for more than five seconds with wood laminate or tiled surfaces.

The current study, undertaken by six final-year biology students led by Aston microbiology professor Anthony Hilton, is likely to only inflame an ongoing debate about this informal rule of food safety, as other studies have found that pathogens transfer themselves to food as soon as that piece of meat or candy hits the kitchen tiles.

The researchers found that the initial impact immediately transferred at least a small proportion of bacteria resident on a floor to just about any type of food. Moist foods left longer than 30 seconds, however, contained up to 10 times more bacteria than food picked up after three seconds. "We believe that additional contact is being made between the moist food and the floor as it settles further onto the floor," Hilton says. Dry foods dropped on the carpet experienced the slowest rate of bacterial migration.

The researchers monitored the transfer of the common bacteria *Escherichia coli* and *Staphylococcus aureus*–the latter of which causes staph infections–from a variety of indoor floor types to toast, pasta, biscuits and a sticky sweet when contact was made from three to 30 seconds.

Hilton and his students had initially been studying the survival and transfer of bacteria on indoor flooring surfaces. The researchers found staph to be the most commonly isolated bacterium on the flooring they examined. They included E. coli in their work because it is a common gut bacterium, often used to model how other gut pathogens–such as salmonella–respond under different conditions. "We introduced time as a factor as a bit of a quirky parameter to explore and didn't really expect it to show anything significant," he says.

The researchers speculate that the contact area made between food and floor surface is significant. "On a smooth surface like tile or laminate the area of contact is greater than when the food is suspended on the tips of the fibers of the carpet," Hilton says. "I think the results from the carpet were the most surprising in transferring very low numbers of bacteria to food and not demonstrating the same effect of time in enhancing transfer."

Most of the 495 people that Hilton and his team surveyed as part of their research had heard of the so-called "five-second rule" but "there was still a good number of people that hadn't," he says. Regardless, 87 percent of survey participants who adhere to the five-second rule said they would eat food dropped on the floor or already have done so. The researchers also found that 81 percent of females surveyed use the rule, compared with 64 percent of males. Hilton says he doesn't have a good explanation for this gender differentiation but points out that this finding is consistent with other research into the five-second rule. One possible conclusion: This is tacit confirmation of another piece of folk wisdom—men are less discerning when it comes to their food's cleanliness.

The research began as a class project, but Hilton says widespread interest in the results has encouraged him to prepare the work for submission to a peer-reviewed journal.

The Aston findings give the dropped-food guideline more legitimacy than have other studies, which tend to consider the rule unadulterated baloney. "We found that bacteria was transferred from tabletops and floors to the food within five seconds—that is, the five-second rule is not an accurate guide when it comes to eating food that has fallen on the floor," said Paul Dawson, a professor in Clemson University's Department of Food, Nutrition and Packaging Sciences, following his 2007 study. That study, published in the *Journal of Applied Microbiology*, was primarily aimed at measuring the persistence of bacteria on surfaces.

The Clemson researchers found that *Salmonella typhimurium* "can be transferred to the foods tested almost immediately on contact" and that the bacteria can survive for up to four weeks on dry surfaces in high-enough populations to be transferred to foods.

A 2003 study by then high-school senior Jillian Clarke, during an internship at the University of Illinois at Urbana–Champaign, likewise found that bacteria transfers to food immediately on contact. In her experiment E. coli moved from floor tiles to cookies and gummy bears well within five seconds.

Most studies, it would seem, discourage adherence to the five-second rule. So, even though Aston's findings suggest that allowing dropped food to linger on the floor certainly increases the risk of bacterial transfer to that fallen indulgence, it's better to think twice before eating anything that touches an unsavory surface—whether it's your kitchen floor or your favorite diner.

About the Author

Larry Greenemeier is the associate editor of technology for Scientific American, *covering a variety of tech-related topics, including biotech, computers, military tech, nanotech and robots.*

Fact or Fiction: Should You Feed a Cold and Starve a Fever?

By Mark Fischetti

Maxims typically date back many years, but "feed a cold, starve a fever" may beat them all. This saying has been traced to a 1574 dictionary by John Withals, which noted that "fasting is a great remedy of fever." The belief is that eating food may help the body generate warmth during a "cold" and that avoiding food may help it cool down when overheated.

But recent medical science says the old saw is wrong. It should be "feed a cold, feed a fever."

Let's take colds first. When your body fights an illness it needs energy, so eating healthy food is helpful. Eating can also help the body generate heat–although wearing an extra layer of clothes or slipping into bed can keep you warm, too. There's no need to overeat, however. The body is quick to turn recently digested food into energy, and it's also efficient at converting stored energy in fat.

The reasons to eat for fever are more interesting. Fever is part of the immune system's attempt to beat the bugs. It raises body temperature, which increases metabolism and results in more calories burned; for each degree of temperature rise, the energy demand increases further. So taking in calories becomes important.

Even more crucial is drinking. Fever dehydrates your system, in part through increased sweating from that elevated temperature. Replacing fluids is therefore critical to helping the body battle the infection. The same is true for combating colds. "You have to make yourself drink fluids, even though all you want to do is collapse," says William Schaffner, chair of the Department of Preventive Medicine at Vanderbilt University School of Medicine.

Dehydration also makes mucus in the nose, throat and lungs dry up, which can then clog sinuses and respiratory tubes. When mucus hardens it becomes more difficult to cough, Schaffner notes, which is our way of trying to expel mucus and the germs it contains.

Staying hydrated helps keep the mucus running, which, even though it may be disgusting, is one of our natural defenses.

The challenge, of course, is that when you're sick you may not feel much like drinking and even less like eating. Loss of appetite is common, and might be part of the body's attempt to focus its energy on pounding the pathogens. Given the wisdom noted above, Schaffner says, don't force yourself to eat if you don't feel like it. "But drink," he adds. "It's the liquids that are important." Avoid caffeine and alcohol. Caffeine enhances dehydration. So does alcohol, and it is also a depressant, holding us down.

What about some other common conceptions for beating colds and fevers, such as eating chicken soup? Chicken soup doesn't possess any magic ingredients, but it has calories as well as the all-important liquids again. The warm vapor rising from the bowl can also moisten and loosen dried mucus. The same goes for vapor from hot tea, with or without lemon or honey. Taking a hot shower can soften mucus, too–and if you dare, you can get rid of it by gently blowing your nose one nostril at a time while you're in there.

Supplements are dubious at best. The data from studies about taking vitamin C are inconclusive, as they are for zinc. Solid studies of echinacea show no benefit. If there's any positive effect at all from any of these compounds, it is very small, Schaffner concludes.

Over-the-counter remedies may or may not help, but that's a whole 'nother story. They can relieve symptoms but they do not kill off viruses or bacteria. Cold and fever germs usually run their course, and the immune system eventually gets the upper hand. In the meantime, drink drink drink. And sleep as much as you can, to give your body the rest it needs to fight the good fight.

About the Author

Mark Fischetti has been a senior editor at Scientific American *for 17 years and has covered sustainability issues, including climate, weather, environment, energy, food, water, biodiversity, population, and more. He assigns and edits feature articles, commentaries and news by journalists and scientists and also writes in those formats. He edits History, the magazine's department looking at science advances throughout time. He was founding managing editor of two spinoff magazines:* Scientific American Mind *and* Scientific American Earth 3.0. *His 2001 freelance article for the magazine, "Drowning New Orleans," predicted the widespread disaster that a storm like Hurricane Katrina would impose on the city. His video* What Happens to Your Body after You Die?, *has more than 12 million views on YouTube. Fischetti has written freelance articles for the* New York Times, Sports Illustrated, Smithsonian, Technology Review, Fast Company, *and many others. He co-authored the book* Weaving the Web *with Tim Berners-Lee, inventor of the World Wide Web, which tells the real story of how the Web was created. He also co-authored* The New Killer Diseases *with microbiologist Elinor Levy. Fischetti is a former managing editor of* IEEE Spectrum Magazine *and of* Family Business Magazine. *He has a physics degree and has twice served as the Attaway Fellow in Civic Culture at Centenary College of Louisiana, which awarded him an honorary doctorate. In 2021 he received the American Geophysical Union's Robert C. Cowen Award for Sustained Achievement in Science Journalism, which celebrates a career of outstanding reporting on the Earth and space sciences. He has appeared on NBC's Meet the Press, CNN, the History Channel, NPR News and many news radio stations. Follow Fischetti on X (formerly Twitter) @markfischetti*

Fact or Fiction: Raw Veggies are Healthier than Cooked Ones

By Sushma Subramanian

Cooking is crucial to our diets. It helps us digest food without expending huge amounts of energy. It softens food, such as cellulose fiber and raw meat, that our small teeth, weak jaws and digestive systems aren't equipped to handle. And while we might hear from raw foodists that cooking kills vitamins and minerals in food (while also denaturing enzymes that aid digestion), it turns out raw vegetables are not always healthier.

A study published in *The British Journal of Nutrition* last year found that a group of 198 subjects who followed a strict raw food diet had normal levels of vitamin A and relatively high levels of beta-carotene (an antioxidant found in dark green and yellow fruits and vegetables), but low levels of the antioxidant lycopene.

Lycopene is a red pigment found predominantly in tomatoes and other rosy fruits such as watermelon, pink guava, red bell pepper and papaya. Several studies conducted in recent years (at Harvard Medical School, among others) have linked high intake of lycopene with a lower risk of cancer and heart attacks. Rui Hai Liu, an associate professor of food science at Cornell University who has researched lycopene, says that it may be an even more potent antioxidant than vitamin C.

One 2002 study he did (published in the *Journal of Agriculture and Food Chemistry*) found that cooking actually boosts the amount of lycopene in tomatoes. He tells *Scientific American* that the level of one type of lycopene, cis-lycopene, in tomatoes rose 35 percent after he cooked them for 30 minutes at 190.4 degrees Fahrenheit (88 degrees Celsius). The reason, he says: the heat breaks down the plants' thick cell walls and aids the body's uptake of some nutrients that are bound to those cell walls.

Cooked carrots, spinach, mushrooms, asparagus, cabbage, peppers and many other vegetables also supply more antioxidants, such as carotenoids and ferulic acid, to the body than they do when raw, Liu says. At least, that is, if they're boiled or steamed. A January 2008 report in the *Journal of Agriculture and Food Chemistry* said that boiling and steaming better preserves antioxidants, particularly carotenoid, in carrots, zucchini and broccoli, than frying, though boiling was deemed the best. The researchers studied the impact of the various cooking techniques on compounds such as carotenoids, ascorbic acid and polyphenols.

Deep fried foods are notorious sources of free radicals, caused by oil being continuously oxidized when it is heated at high temperatures. These radicals, which are highly reactive because they have at least one unpaired electron, can injure cells in the body. The antioxidants in the oil and the vegetables get used up during frying in stabilizing the cycle of oxidation.

Another study published in the *Journal of Agricultural and Food Chemistry* in 2002 showed that cooking carrots increases their level of beta-carotene. Beta-carotene belongs to a group of antioxidant substances called carotenoids, which give fruits and vegetables their red, yellow, and orange colorings. The body converts beta-carotene into vitamin A, which plays an important role in vision, reproduction, bone growth and regulating the immune system.

The downside of cooking veggies, Liu says: it can destroy the vitamin C in them. He found that vitamin C levels declined by 10 percent in tomatoes cooked for two minutes–and 29 percent in tomatoes that were cooked for half an hour at 190.4 degrees F (88 degrees C). The reason is that Vitamin C, which is highly unstable, is easily degraded through oxidation, exposure to heat (it can increase the rate at which vitamin C reacts with oxygen in the air) and through cooking in water (it dissolves in water).

Liu notes, however, that the trade-off may be worth it since vitamin C is prevalent in far more fruits and vegetables than is lycopene. Among them: broccoli, oranges, cauliflower, kale and carrots. Besides, cooked vegetables retain some of their vitamin C content.

That said, research shows that some veggies, including broccoli, are healthier raw rather than cooked. According to a study in the *Journal of Agricultural and Food Chemistry* in November 2007, heat damages the enzyme myrosinase, which breaks down glucosinates (compounds derived from glucose and an amino acid) in broccoli into a compound known as sulforaphane.

Research published in the journal *Carcinogenesis* in December 2008 found that sulforaphane might block the proliferation of and kill precancerous cells. A 2002 study in *The Proceedings of the National Academy of Sciences* also found that sulforaphane may help fight the bacterium Helicobacter pylori, which causes ulcers and increases a person's risk of stomach cancer.

On the other hand, indole, an organic compound, is formed when certain plants, particularly cruciferous vegetables such as broccoli, cauliflower and cabbage, are cooked. According to research in *The Journal of Nutrition* in 2001, indole helps kill precancerous cells before they turn malignant. And while boiling carrots was found to increase carotenoid levels, another study found that it leads to a total loss of polyphenols, a group of chemicals found in raw carrots. Specific polyphenols have been shown to have antioxidant properties and to reduce the risk of cardiovascular disease and cancer, according to a 2005 report in *The American Journal of Clinical Nutrition*.

Comparing the healthfulness of raw and cooked food is complicated, and there are still many mysteries surrounding how the different molecules in plants interact with the human body. The bottom line, says Liu, is to eat your veggies and fruits no matter how they're prepared.

"We cook them so they taste better," Liu says. "If they taste better, we're more likely to eat them." And that's the whole idea.

About the Author

Sushma Subramanian is a freelance science writer and an assistant professor of journalism at the University of Mary Washington.

What the Evidence Says about Fluoride in Drinking Water

By Saima S. Iqbal

Municipalities across the U.S. have been safely adding fluoride to their tap water for decades, and reams of data prove the mineral has worked wonders in strengthening enamel and preventing tooth decay. But communities could soon start removing or lowering levels of fluoride in public drinking water as misinformation about its purported harms gains dangerous momentum among media outlets and a growing number of prominent political figures.

This month Robert F. Kennedy, Jr.–President-elect Donald Trump's current nominee for the next secretary of the U.S. Department of Health and Human Services (HHS)–fueled a fluoride furor on social media when he called the mineral "industrial waste." Kennedy, a former presidential candidate, claimed fluoride exposure could lead to arthritis, bone cancer, thyroid disease, IQ loss and neurodevelopmental conditions. He has said he would advise against adding it to tap water–a practice that currently reaches more than 209 million Americans.

It remains unclear whether the incoming Trump administration *could* effectively ban water fluoridation: current laws let state and local governments make the decision. But at the federal level, fluoridation opponents could deploy the Safe Drinking Water Act, which regulates water contaminants nationally. They could also take advantage of a recent federal court decision: In September a California district court judge ordered the Environmental Protection Agency to set stricter regulations on tap water fluoride levels, arguing that the HHS's national concentration recommendations might lower children's IQ scores. But the judge leaned heavily on a recent controversial scientific report that had been rejected twice in peer review for a lack of rigor.

"His conclusion was misguided–and an overreach," says Charlotte W. Lewis, a pediatrician and dental care researcher at the University of Washington School of Medicine. She notes that widely accepted research shows water fluoridation to be an effective disease-prevention measure, especially for people in communities with less access to dental care.

The EPA is currently deciding whether to appeal the district court's order. But the Trump administration could sway the outcome by reversing any EPA decision made under outgoing president Joe Biden. And Kennedy's rhetoric alone could persuade some individuals or communities to avoid fluoride-containing water. Since 2010 more than 170 U.S. cities, towns and counties have voted to halt fluoridation, according to one antifluoride group's records. More are expected to follow suit: local lawmakers in Kentucky and Georgia recently sought to reverse their state's fluoride mandate.

Below, *Scientific American* wades into the history and science of fluoridated drinking water by addressing some common questions.

Why Do Public Health Agencies Recommend Water Fluoridation?

Towns and cities across the U.S. began adding fluoride to drinking water in the late 1940s, after studies of thousands of kids showed that communities with naturally occurring low levels of fluoride in their water supply experienced dramatically less tooth decay. The mineral–which is found in rocks, soil and water–prevents and repairs enamel erosion caused by oral bacteria. Today water utilities dissolve trace amounts of one of three fluoride-containing chemical additives in tap water. The U.S. Centers for Disease Control and Prevention's recommended concentration is 0.7 milligram of fluoride per liter of water (an amount that is equivalent to about three drops of liquid per 55-gallon barrel). Facilities are required to monitor and report fluoride levels on a daily and monthly basis.

Fluoridating city water supplies initially slashed kids' cavity rates by 50 to 70 percent and lowered adults' rates by 20 to 40 percent, vastly reducing tooth pain, infection and loss. But now that toothpaste and beverage companies also add fluoride to their products, the benefits of community water fluoridation have decreased: several credible studies estimate that fluoridated water now reduces child and adult tooth decay by about 25 percent. The CDC and the American Dental Association emphasize that this still remains a significant benefit–and meaningfully shrinks dental health disparities.

A 2022 KFF poll found that dental services were the most common form of health care that adults put off because of high costs. Today at least 68.5 million Americans lack dental insurance, according to a 2023 survey by the CareQuest Institute for Oral Health. Having multiple fluoride sources offers people's teeth much needed protection, says Susan Fisher-Owens, a University of California, San Francisco, Medical Center pediatrician, who studies barriers to children's dental health. For people who cannot regularly access fluoride-containing dental products, fluoridated tap water provides a crucial–and cost-effective–baseline amount of the mineral. "The beauty of community water fluoridation is that it's equal access," she says.

Can Fluoridated Water Pose Risks to Health?

In children who are still developing mature teeth, chronic fluoride overexposure can cause dental fluorosis, a condition that disrupts the uniform color and texture of enamel. Mild and moderate cases include harmless, albeit unattractive, white streaks or patches. Severe cases cause more conspicuous reddish-brown stains and pitted enamel, which can raise the risk of tooth decay.

To prevent severe dental fluorosis, the EPA requires public water systems to warn community members when their water sources exceed a fluoride level of two milligrams per liter (2 mg/L). That is around three times higher than the 0.7 mg/L concentration recommended by the HHS. Fluoride also appears in some foods, beverages and dental products but at small amounts that do not meaningfully contribute to a risk for dental fluorosis–except in cases where children regularly swallow large amounts of toothpaste. (Cute marketing and candylike flavors can sometimes encourage this.)

At extremely high concentrations–around twice the level that causes severe dental fluorosis–fluoride can accumulate in bones, weakening them and causing joint pain. But skeletal fluorosis is exceedingly rare in the U.S., which bans public water supplies from containing such high concentrations.

An apparent association between excessive fluoride exposure and lower IQ scores in children emerged in the 1990s and early 2000s from studies of rural villages in China, where wells had fluoride levels high enough to damage bones. But such findings do not apply to U.S. communities, which allow far less fluoride in water. The studies were also small and poorly designed, failing to account for pervasive contaminants produced by burning coal and peat. Continued research could not identify a clear mechanism that explains how fluoride might damage the developing brain. This prompted many scientists to question the link, Lewis says.

Then, in 2019, a *JAMA Pediatrics* study on pregnant people in Canada raised concerns about fluoride levels close to those that are currently recommended in the U.S. The small study found that if participants had higher fluoride levels in their urine during pregnancy (around 0.4 mg/L) and gave birth to a boy, on average, their son had slightly lower IQ test scores by the time he was three to four years old. (This finding did not apply to daughters.) But fluoride levels in a pregnant person's urine do not indicate how much of the mineral that individual or their embryo or fetus actually takes in, explains Loc Do, an oral epidemiologist at University of Queensland in Australia, who wasn't involved in the paper. The researchers also neglected to administer IQ tests in a standardized way, potentially skewing their results, and did not examine other factors correlated with a child's IQ, such as maternal breastfeeding.

These studies still roused alarm, leading the HHS's National Toxicology Program (NTP) to launch a review of the science in 2016. Its report, released in August 2024, claimed to have determined, "with moderate confidence," that fluoridated water at concentrations of 1.5 mg/L–twice the average level found in U.S. water supplies–harms children's IQ. (The report's authors noted that the review did not address currently recommended exposure levels or "assess the benefits of the use of fluorides in oral health or provide a risk-benefit analysis.")

But before it was even released, the agency's report twice failed to pass scientific review from the National Academies of Sciences, Engineering, and Medicine, an independent research body. And the American Dental Association and the American Academy of Pediatrics criticized the latest report for generating conclusions from a small and weak body of research—and for omitting much larger studies that showed no neurocognitive threat at all from community water fluoridation.

"I wish we could put the genie back in the bottle on NTP," says Steven Levy, a dental health care researcher at the University of Iowa. Despite having "some fundamental flaws," the agency's report has swayed many laypeople and some scientists who are unfamiliar with fluoride research. "Coming from such a well-regarded National Institutes of Health organization gives [the report] more credibility than it should have," he says.

As a case in point, Do recently led a rigorous study of more than 2,500 kids in Australia that found that drinking water with fluoride as concentrated as 1.1 mg/L didn't negatively affect children's cognitive, emotional or behavioral development in their first five years of life. And a 2023 meta-analysis by Fisher-Owens and other dental experts, tasked with the same work as the National Toxicology Program, concluded that fluoride exposures up to 1.5 mg/L had no measurable effect on children's IQ.

What Might Happen if More People or Local Governments Reject Water Fluoridation?

Studies show communities that cease water fluoridation generally see more cavities in kids—and consequently incur higher dental bills. But the extent to which fluoride removal affects a population's health varies because of factors such as diet and local dental practices.

After Israel nixed water fluoridation in 2014, for example, kids aged three to five required twice as many dental procedures as before. A comparison of two cities in Alberta, meanwhile, found that, among second-graders who grew up without any exposure to fluoridated water, the prevalence of cavities was 10 percent higher than that of their neighbors who were exposed. And children in Alaska who were younger than six years old and on Medicaid (the federal-state insurance program that covers most people with low incomes) developed an average of one additional cavity per year, requiring $300 more in dental care.

Public health researchers expect the brunt of fluoride removal to fall on people with low incomes, pre-existing dental conditions, or physical or cognitive disabilities. Levy believes that many healthy people would likely be able to maintain adequate dental health or to afford occasional cavity treatment, but he emphasizes that marginalized people tend to have fewer prevention and treatment options for tooth decay. Socioeconomic barriers can make it difficult for a person to regularly brush and floss their teeth, maintain a healthy diet or access dental care.

Local governments could mitigate negative health outcomes by distributing free toothbrushes, toothpaste tubes and bottles of fluoridated water to people who request them. Without coordinated action, however, people in communities that remove fluoride from the public supply will need to take more diligent care of their teeth.

Experts underscored the importance of brushing twice a day with fluoridated toothpaste, limiting sugar intake, particularly in the form of sodas and juices, and consulting a dentist or pediatrician about additional preventative measures. The U.S. Preventive Services Task Force–an independent panel of primary care experts–currently recommends that children under age five who do not have access to sufficiently fluoridated water receive oral fluoride supplements. Both children and adults can also benefit from receiving regular fluoride varnishes (a temporary enamel coating of highly concentrated fluoride) or plastic sealants (a semipermanent protective layer for tooth surfaces and crevices) at the dentist's office.

Some specialized water filtration methods, such as reverse osmosis and the use of activated alumina, are designed to capture lead and other contaminants and can also sift out fluoride. (Common activated carbon filters such as Brita and Pur filters do not remove the mineral.) Experts say drinking only filtered or purified water may potentially cause insufficient fluoride intake, but occasional use isn't a health concern.

Some dental products do not contain fluoride, such as hydroxyapatite toothpaste, which is approved in Canada and Europe. Hydroxyapatite has received some hype in American media outlets, and small and limited studies show it to be similarly effective to fluoride toothpaste. Other experimental fluorideless toothpastes, however, have shown positive results that aren't replicated in larger trials, says Gary Slade, a dental health epidemiologist at the University of North Carolina Adams School of Dentistry. "Maybe in five years, I'll be giving [hydroxyapatite] a thumbs-up," Slade says. "For now, I'd like to see some more studies."

Public health experts also worry the current political frenzy around fluoride could feed more misinformation about effective health practices–including vaccinations. "Uncritical acceptance of these methodologically deficient studies will only encourage more poor-quality studies," says Jay Kumar, a retired epidemiologist, who co-authored the 2023 meta-analysis. "If we keep perpetuating bad science, people are going to stop trusting government reports."

About the Author

Saima S. Iqbal is a former Scientific American *news intern. She specializes in health and medicine and is based in New York City.*

Section 6: Our Planet and People

No, You Can't See the Great Wall of China from Space

By Phil Plait

When I was a mere lad, probably in middle school, I remember a friend telling me that the Apollo astronauts could see the Great Wall of China from the moon.

If someone told me that now, I'd know almost instinctively that this claim is baloney. Of course, back then when I was a lot less skeptical (and didn't know anything about optics or physics or ocular biology), my reaction was, "Cool!"

But I do know about those topics now and have some experience dealing with seeing objects from space. So let's look at just why that claim can't be true.

The basic problem (as with so many "you can see X from space"-type statements) is resolution. This is a term astronomers use for the ability to distinguish two closely spaced objects, as opposed to seeing them so close together that they merge into a single dot. You likely have experience with this: driving on a highway at night, you'll see an oncoming car's headlights as one single light source until the car gets close enough to reveal there are, in fact, two.

Resolution is usually expressed in terms of an angle that is determined by the size of the object and its distance from the observer. For a concrete example, the moon is about 3,500 kilometers wide and 380,000 km away from Earth; do the math and you'll find that the moon appears to be about 0.5 degrees across (where, as you may recall, a circle–say, the horizon around you–is 360 degrees in circumference).

The average human eye offers a visual resolution of about one arcminute (there are 60 arcminutes in a degree); someone with very keen vision might be able to resolve an object half that size. The moon is much larger than this in the sky, so it looks like a disk with features that are easily seen.

What about the Great Wall of China, though? While it is very long, this structure is actually quite narrow. One of the wider parts might be 10 meters. Can something that size be seen from the moon?

At that distance, the Great Wall would appear as a line one ten-thousandth of an arcminute thick. Resolving that feature would be roughly the equivalent of seeing a human hair from a kilometer away with your unaided eyes. I think you'll agree that that's flatly impossible!

But let's modify the claim somewhat: Say now we're in low-Earth orbit, watching our planet rolling along from the cupola of the International Space Station (ISS). That's a perch roughly 400 km above Earth's surface, so from there the Great Wall would appear about 0.1 arcminute in width. So even then, it's still too small to see by eye!

There's still a chance, however. Our eyes can be a little better at seeing objects that are very narrow if they're very long and have high contrast with the surrounding environment. Orbiting astronauts can see roads across deserts, for example, and the wakes of seafaring ships. Does that help here?

Sadly, no. The Great Wall is made of stone that generally doesn't contrast well against the terrain, and it tends to curve as it follows the landscape, especially near steep cliffs and hills.

And we know this empirically, too: astronauts have tried to see it but have never reliably done so. (Orbital snapshots that show any details are captured using a telephoto lens, which has a much higher resolution than the human eye.) Even China's first taikonaut, Yang Liwei, said he couldn't see it from orbit, and certainly national pride would have motivated him to try.

I'll note that there may be certain conditions when it really *is* detectable from orbit. For example, when the sun is low in the sky at sunrise or sunset, the wall can cast a long shadow, revealing its presence. But that's not really the same as *seeing* the wall itself, is it?

Well then, what about other human-made objects? The Great Wall is long, but we've certainly built structures that are bulkier.

The pyramids in Egypt are obvious candidates. The Great Pyramid of Giza is about 230 meters across on each side of its base, making it easily big enough to resolve by eye from low-Earth orbit. The dusty stone doesn't provide a lot of contrast with the surrounding sand, but more contrast can come from the play of light across the structure itself: at low sun angles, half the pyramid is lit and half is in shadow, distinguishing it against the sandy landscape. One former NASA astronaut, Leroy Chiao, claims to have seen two of the pyramids, while others have reportedly tried but failed.

NASA claims the Three Gorges Dam in China can be seen from space. I haven't seen any reports of astronauts actually spotting it, but it *should* be *possible*. The dam is immense: it's more than 100 meters across at its base and 2.3 km long. Its tan color contrasts with the blue waters of the Yangtze River it spans and shows up easily in photographs taken by astronauts using a telephoto lens.

It's worth noting that you don't necessarily need to resolve an object to see it. Stars are great examples. While they're huge, some millions of kilometers in diameter, they are also fantastically distant; even the closest (besides the sun) is more than 40 trillion km away. They are all unresolved dots by eye yet easily visible (at least at night). In this case, though, they're *bright*. Even something unresolved can be seen if it's emitting or reflecting enough light.

That's why city lights can be easily seen from orbit and are likely even visible from the moon under some circumstances. One difficulty is that the brightly lit lunar landscape can ruin the view—astronauts on the moon had difficulty seeing stars through the glare, even though the sky itself was black. Also, Earth in the moon's sky is far brighter than the moon is from Earth, which can make city lights more difficult to tease out. Perhaps if a lunar astronaut hid in the shadow of a big boulder and Earth was in a thin crescent phase, cities might be faintly visible on our planet's night side. That would be a fun experiment to try, and I hope future lunar explorers give it a shot.

And while we're thinking about all this, let's turn the tables: Can you resolve the ISS from the ground? Its light is certainly visible and can be brighter than Venus at times.

It turns out that the answer is *yes* (kind of). The ISS is about 100 meters across, which means that it can be slightly less than one arcminute in size when it passes directly overhead and is therefore closest to an observer. So someone with keen vision could see it as just barely more than a dot. I'll note that with even modest binoculars, you can easily see it as a stubby line; I've done so myself.

And finally, while individual human-made objects are difficult to see from space, our effects on the planet are not. In his book *An Astronaut's Guide to Life on Earth*, Canadian astronaut Chris Hadfield wrote that from the ISS, he could see the effects of deforestation in Madagascar as soil was dumped into the ocean. Wildfires, exacerbated by climate change, have plumes that can easily be spotted. And, of course, our cities glow fiercely from just a few hundred kilometers above.

From space we are tiny—but our impact is not.

About the Author

Phil Plait is a professional astronomer and science communicator in Virginia. His column for Scientific American, *The Universe, covers all things space. He writes the* Bad Astronomy Newsletter. *Follow him online.*

Top 10 Myths about Sustainability

By Michael D. Lemonick

When a word becomes so popular you begin hearing it everywhere, in all sorts of marginally related or even unrelated contexts, it means one of two things. Either the word has devolved into a meaningless cliché, or it has real conceptual heft. "Green" (or, even worse, "going green") falls squarely into the first category. But "sustainable," which at first conjures up a similarly vague sense of environmental virtue, actually belongs in the second. True, you hear it applied to everything from cars to agriculture to economics. But that's because the concept of sustainability is at its heart so simple that it legitimately applies to all these areas and more.

Despite its simplicity, however, sustainability is a concept people have a hard time wrapping their minds around. To help, *Scientific American Earth 3.0* has consulted with several experts on the topic to find out what kinds of misconceptions they most often encounter. The result is this take on the top 10 myths about sustainability. And after this introduction, it's clear which myth has to come first....

Myth 1: Nobody knows what sustainability really means.

That's not even close to being true. By all accounts, the modern sense of the word entered the lexicon in 1987 with the publication of *Our Common Future*, by the United Nations World Commission on Environment and Development (also known as the Brundtland commission after its chair, Norwegian diplomat Gro Harlem Brundtland). That report defined sustainable development as "development that meets the needs of the present without compromising the ability of future generations to meet their own needs." Or, in the words of countless kindergarten teachers, "Don't take more than your share."

Note that the definition says nothing about protecting the environment, even though the words "sustainable" and "sustainability" issue mostly from the mouths of environmentalists. That point leads to the second myth....

Myth 2: Sustainability is all about the environment.
The sustainability movement itself–not just the word–also dates to the Brundtland commission report. Originally, its focus was on finding ways to let poor nations catch up to richer ones in terms of standard of living. That goal meant giving disadvantaged countries better access to natural resources, including water, energy and food–all of which come, one way or another, from the environment. "The economy," says Anthony Cortese, founder and president of the sustainability education organization Second Nature, "is a wholly owned subsidiary of the biosphere. The biosphere provides everything that makes life possible, assimilates our waste or converts it back into something we can use."

If too many of us use resources inefficiently or generate waste too quickly for the environment to absorb and process, future generations obviously won't be able to meet their needs. Says Paul Hawken, the author (his latest book is *Blessed Unrest: How the Largest Movement in the World Came into Being, and Why No One Saw it Coming*) and entrepreneur (he's a co-founder of the Smith & Hawken garden tools company) who helped to found the sustainability movement: "We have an economy where we steal the future, sell it in the present, and call it GDP [gross domestic product]."

If people continue to pour carbon dioxide (CO_2) into the air, for example, we won't necessarily exhaust resources (there's plenty of coal still in the ground), but we will change the climate in ways that could very likely impose huge burdens on future generations. The same, of course, goes for the poisonous by-products other than CO_2 from all kinds of human activity, from manufacturing to mining to energy generation to agriculture, that get dumped onto the land and into streams, oceans and the atmosphere.

The nonenvironmental rationales for sustainability get a little squishier when we talk about intangibles, such as the beauty of nature or the value of wilderness. "In wildness is the preservation of the world," wrote Henry David Thoreau; the national parks movement that began in the U.S. at the end of the 19th century and has since spread internationally springs from that idea. In modern terms, because humans evolved in a nontechnological world, we seem to need some connection to nature to be content. That concept is tough to prove scientifically. Nevertheless, says Nancy Gabriel, program director at the Sustainability Institute in Hartland, Vt., "If you look at Western society, you have huge rates of depression, isolation, [and] people who are disenfranchised. I think that reconnecting to the land is an important way of reestablishing a basic level of happiness." That kind of intangible connection has led towns, cities and states all over the U.S., but especially in built-up areas, to preserve land for open space.

A related but separate myth is....

Myth 3: "Sustainable" is a synonym for "green."

Although there's a fair amount of overlap between the terms, "green" usually suggests a preference for the natural over the artificial. With some six billion people on the planet today, and another three billion expected by the middle of the century, society cannot hope to give them a comfortable standard of living without a heavy dependence on technology. Electric cars, wind turbines and solar cells are the antithesis of natural–but they allow people to get around, warm their houses and cook their food with renewable resources (or at least, a much smaller input of nonrenewables) while emitting fewer noxious chemicals.

It's probably more difficult to see nuclear power as sustainable. Unlike the other alternative energy sources, it has long been anathema to environmentalists, largely because of the problem of storing radioactive waste. But nuclear reactors are also a highly efficient source of power, emit no pollutant gases and–with some types, anyway–can be designed to generate minimal waste and to be essentially meltdown-proof. That's why Patrick Moore, a co-founder of Greenpeace, has become a nuclear booster and why many other environmentalists are beginning–sometimes grudgingly–to entertain the idea of embracing nuclear. Calling it green would be a stretch. Calling it sustainable is much less of one.

Myth 4: It's all about recycling.
"I get that a lot," says Shana Weber, the manager of sustainability at Princeton University. "For some reason, recycling was the enduring message that came out of the environmental movement in the early 1970s." And of course, recycling is important: reusing metals, paper, wood and plastics rather than tossing them reduces the need to extract raw materials from the ground, forests and fossil-fuel deposits. More efficient use of pretty much anything is a step in the direction of sustainability. But it is just a piece of the puzzle. "I deal with the people who run the recycling program here," Weber notes, "but also with purchasing, dining services, the people who clean the buildings. The most important areas by far in terms of sustainability are energy and transportation." If you think you are living sustainably because you recycle, she says, you need to think again.

Myth 5: Sustainability is too expensive.
If there is an 800-pound gorilla in the room of sustainability, this myth is it. That's because, as Gabriel observes, "there's a grain of truth to it." But only a grain. "It's only true in the short term in certain circumstances," Cortese says, "but certainly not in the long term." The truth lies in the fact that if you already have an unsustainable system in place—a factory or a transportation system, for example, or a furnace in your house, an incandescent lightbulb in your lamp or a Hummer in your driveway—you have to spend some money up front to switch to a more sustainable technology.

In general, governments and companies can take that step more easily than individuals can. "Over the past seven years," Cortese explains, "DuPont has made investments that have reduced its greenhouse gas emissions by 72 percent over 1990 levels. They've saved $2 billion." The Pentagon is determined to cut its energy use by a third, both to save money and to reduce its dependence on risky foreign oil supplies.

Myth 6: Sustainability means lowering our standard of living.
Not at all true. It does mean that we have to do more with less, but as Hawken argues, "Once we start to organize ourselves and

innovate within that mind-set, the breakthroughs are extraordinary. They will allow us to achieve greatly superior rates of resource productivity, which in turn allow us to be prosperous, fed, clad, secure." Moreover, he and others maintain that the innovation at the heart of sustainable living will be a powerful economic engine. "Addressing climate change," he says, "is the biggest job creation program there is."

Myth 7: Consumer choices and grassroots activism, not government intervention, offer the fastest, most efficient routes to sustainability.

Popular grassroots actions are helpful and ultimately necessary. But progress on some reforms, such as curbing CO_2 emissions, can only happen quickly if central authorities commit to making it happen. That is why tax credits, mandatory fuel-efficiency standards and the like are pretty much inevitable. That conclusion drives free-market evangelists crazy, but they operate on the assumption that wasteful use of resources and the destruction of the environment is without cost, which is demonstrably untrue.

To cite just one example, economic devastation is very likely under even the mildest plausible climate change scenarios, in the form of disruptions to agriculture from shifts in rainfall patterns and growing zones; densely populated coastal areas will be rendered unlivable as sea level rises, and so on. Yet the price currently being charged to people who add greenhouse gases to the atmosphere is zero. Putting a per-ton tax on carbon emissions would be wildly unpopular, but it would for the first time account for the real costs of unsustainable energy use.

Free-market purists also argue that with respect to the depletion of natural resources, rising prices will automatically push people into more efficient behavior. True enough–but the transition can be painful and disruptive. The primary reason U.S. automakers are in such trouble is that they have been depending for years on high-profit, gas-guzzling SUVs. When the price of oil shot up last year, the market for big cars plummeted (gas prices have only come down since then in the face of a worldwide recession, which hasn't helped the auto industry). So car buyers may have changed their behavior, but only at the cost of potential disaster for some of America's biggest companies and their employees.

Still, rising energy prices have had the effect of again galvanizing research into wind, solar and other alternatives–and if you leave economic disruption aside, we can at least count on car companies to make more efficient vehicles and on utilities to find more sustainable sources of energy. But that outcome may reflect another myth....

Myth 8: New technology is always the answer.

Not necessarily. During his presidential campaign, Barack Obama made the tactical mistake of pointing out that proper tire inflation could save Americans millions of gallons of gasoline through better fuel economy. The Republicans ridiculed him, just as they did President Jimmy Carter for appearing on TV in a sweater during the energy crisis of the late 1970s. Both Carter and Obama were right, however (California's Republican governor Arnold Schwarzenegger has called for proper tire inflation as well).

In other words, sometimes existing technology can make a huge difference. Sometimes it takes a creative business model. Israeli entrepreneur Shai Agassi, for example, wants to electrify the world's car fleet–widely acknowledged as a big step toward cutting down carbon emissions–not by inventing a battery that gets 200 miles on a charge but by inventing a better system for letting drivers go as far as they want without recharging. His proposal, which has been adopted on a pilot basis by Israel and Denmark, would create battery exchange stations along highways, analogous to the gas canister exchanges that people now use for barbecue grills. What do you do if you are out on the road and your battery is running low? You pull into a station, your dead battery is swapped for a fully charged one and you're on the road again in a few minutes.

"He's delivering distance, not better batteries," says Mark Lee, CEO of the London consulting firm SustainAbility. "There's an Italian utility that's selling its customers hot water, not energy to heat water. It's a different way of measuring, and it gives the company an incentive to be more efficient so it can be more profitable."

Myth 9: Sustainability is ultimately a population problem.
This is not a myth, but it represents a false solution. Every environmental problem is ultimately a population problem. If the world's population were only 100 million people, we would be hard-pressed to generate enough waste to overwhelm nature's cleanup systems. We could dump all our trash in a landfill in some remote area, and nobody would notice.

Population experts agree that the best way to limit population is to educate women and raise the standard of living generally in developing countries. But that strategy cannot possibly happen quickly enough to put a dent in the population on any useful timescale. The U.N. projects that the planet will have to sustain another 2.6 billion people by 2050. But even at the current population level of 6.5 billion, we're using up resources at an unsustainable rate. There is no way to reduce the population significantly without trampling egregiously on individual rights (as China has done with its one-child policy), encouraging mass suicide or worse. None of those proposals seems preferable to focusing directly on less wasteful use of resources.

Myth 10: Once you understand the concept, living sustainably is a breeze to figure out.
All too often, a choice that seems sustainable turns out on closer examination to be problematic. Probably the best current example is the rush to produce ethanol for fuel from corn. Corn is a renewable resource–you can harvest it and grow more, roughly indefinitely. So replacing gasoline with corn ethanol seems like a great idea. Until you do a thorough analysis, that is, and see how energy-intensive the cultivation and harvesting of corn and its conversion into ethanol really are.

One might get a bit more energy out of the ethanol than was sunk into making it, which could still make ethanol more sustainable than gasoline in principle, but that's not the end of the problem. Diverting corn to make ethanol means less corn is left to feed livestock and people, which drives up the cost of food. That consequence leads to turning formerly fallow land–including, in some cases, rain forest in places such as Brazil—into farmland, which in turn releases lots of carbon dioxide into the atmosphere. Eventually, over many decades, the energy benefit from burning ethanol would make up for that forest loss. But by then, climate change would have progressed so far that it might not help.

You cannot really declare any practice "sustainable" until you have done a complete life-cycle analysis of its environmental costs. Even then, technology and public policy keep evolving, and that evolution can lead to unforeseen and unintended consequences. The admirable goal of living sustainably requires plenty of thought on an ongoing basis.

About the Author

Michael D. Lemonick is a freelance writer, as well as former chief opinion editor at Scientific American and a former senior science writer at Time. *His most recent book is* The Perpetual Now: A Story of Amnesia, Memory and Love *(Doubleday, 2017). Lemonick also teaches science journalism at Princeton University.*

The Theory That Men Evolved to Hunt and Women Evolved to Gather Is Wrong

By Cara Ocobock & Sarah Lacy

Even if you're not an anthropologist, you've probably encountered one of this field's most influential notions, known as Man the Hunter. The theory proposes that hunting was a major driver of human evolution and that men carried this activity out to the exclusion of women. It holds that human ancestors had a division of labor, rooted in biological differences between males and females, in which males evolved to hunt and provide and females tended to children and domestic duties. It assumes that males are physically superior to females and that pregnancy and child-rearing reduce or eliminate a female's ability to hunt.

Man the Hunter has dominated the study of human evolution for nearly half a century and pervaded popular culture. It is represented in museum dioramas and textbook figures, Saturday morning cartoons and feature films. The thing is, it's wrong.

Mounting evidence from exercise science indicates that women are physiologically better suited than men to endurance efforts such as running marathons. This advantage bears on questions about hunting because a prominent hypothesis contends that early humans are thought to have pursued prey on foot over long distances until the animals were exhausted. Furthermore, the fossil and archaeological records, as well as ethnographic studies of modern-day hunter-gatherers, indicate that women have a long history of hunting game. We still have much to learn about female athletic performance and the lives of prehistoric women. Nevertheless, the data we do have signal that it is time to bury Man the Hunter for good.

The theory rose to prominence in 1968, when anthropologists Richard B. Lee and Irven DeVore published Man the Hunter, an edited collection of scholarly papers presented at a 1966 symposium on contemporary hunter-gatherer societies. The volume drew on ethnographic, archaeological and paleoanthropological evidence to argue that hunting is what drove human evolution and resulted in our suite of unique features. "Man's life as a hunter supplied all the other ingredients for achieving civilization: the genetic variability, the inventiveness, the systems of vocal communication, the coordination of social life," anthropologist William S. Laughlin writes in chapter 33 of the book. Because men were supposedly the ones hunting, proponents of the Man the Hunter theory assumed evolution was acting primarily on men, and women were merely passive beneficiaries of both the meat supply and evolutionary progress.

But *Man the Hunter*'s contributors often ignored evidence, sometimes in their own data, that countered their suppositions. For example, Hitoshi Watanabe focused on ethnographic data about the Ainu, an Indigenous population in northern Japan and its surrounding areas. Although Watanabe documented Ainu women hunting, often with the aid of dogs, he dismissed this finding in his interpretations and placed the focus squarely on men as the primary meat winners. He was superimposing the idea of male superiority through hunting onto the Ainu and into the past.

This fixation on male superiority was a sign of the times not just in academia but in society at large. In 1967, the year between the *Man the Hunter* conference and the publication of the edited volume, 20-year-old Kathrine Switzer entered the Boston Marathon under the name "K. V. Switzer," which obscured her gender. There were no official rules against women entering the race; it just was not done. When officials discovered that Switzer was a woman, race manager Jock Semple attempted to push her physically off the course.

At that time, the conventional wisdom was that women were incapable of completing such a physically demanding task and that attempting to do so could harm their precious reproductive capacities. Scholars following Man the Hunter dogma relied on this belief in women's limited physical capacities and the assumed burden of pregnancy and lactation to argue that only men hunted. Women had children to rear instead.

Today these biased assumptions persist in both the scientific literature and the public consciousness. Granted, women have recently been shown hunting in movies such as *Prey*, the newest installment of the popular Predator franchise, and on cable programs such as *Naked and Afraid* and *Women Who Hunt*. But social media trolls have viciously critiqued and labeled these depictions as part of a politically correct feminist agenda. They insist the creators of such works are trying to rewrite gender roles and evolutionary history in an attempt to co-opt "traditionally masculine" social spheres. Bystanders might be left wondering whether portrayals of women hunters are trying to make the past more inclusive than it really was–or whether Man the Hunter-style assumptions about the past are attempts to project sexism backward in time. Our recent surveys of the physiological and archaeological evidence for hunting capability and sexual division of labor in human evolution answer this question.

Before getting into the evidence, we need to first talk about sex and gender. "Sex" typically refers to biological sex, which can be defined by myriad characteristics such as chromosomes, hormone levels, gonads, external genitalia and secondary sex characteristics. The terms "female" and "male" are often used in relation to biological sex. "Gender" refers to how an individual identifies–woman, man, nonbinary, and so forth. Much of the scientific literature confuses and conflates female/male and woman/man terminology without providing definitions to clarify what it is referring to and why those terms were chosen. For the purpose of describing anatomical and physiological evidence, most of the literature uses "female" and "male," so we use those words here when discussing the results of such studies. For ethnographic and archaeological evidence, we are attempting to reconstruct social roles, for which the terms "woman" and "man" are usually used. Unfortunately, both these word sets assume a binary, which does not exist biologically, psychologically or socially. Sex and gender both exist as a spectrum, but it is difficult to add that nuance when citing the work of others.

It also bears mentioning that much of the research into exercise physiology, paleoanthropology, archaeology and ethnography has historically been conducted by men and focused on males. For example, Ella Smith of the Australian Catholic University and her colleagues found that in studies of nutrition and supplements, only 23 percent of participants were female. Emma Cowley, then at the University of North Carolina at Chapel Hill, and her colleagues found that among published studies focusing on athletic performance, only 6 percent had female-only participants; 31 percent looked exclusively at males. This massive disparity means we still know very little about female athletic performance, training and nutrition, leaving athletic trainers and coaches to treat females mostly as small males. It also means that much of the work we have to rely on to make our physiological arguments about female hunters in prehistory is based on research with small human sample sizes or rodent studies. We hope this state of affairs will inspire the next generation of scientists to ensure that females are represented in such studies. But even with the limited data available to us, we can show that Man the Hunter is a flawed theory and make the case that females in early human communities hunted, too.

From a biological standpoint, there are undeniable differences between females and males. When we discuss these differences, we are typically referring to means, averages of one group compared with another. Means obscure the vast range of variation in humans. For instance, although males tend to be larger and to have bigger hearts and lungs and more muscle mass, there are plenty of females who fall within the typical male range; the inverse is also true.

Overall, females are metabolically better suited for endurance activities, whereas males excel at short, powerful burst-type activities. You can think of it as marathoners (females) versus powerlifters (males). Much of this difference seems to be driven by the powers of the hormone estrogen.

Given the fitness world's persistent touting of the hormone testosterone for athletic success, you'd be forgiven for not knowing that estrogen, which females typically produce more of than males, plays an incredibly important role in athletic performance. It makes sense from an evolutionary standpoint, however. The estrogen receptor–the protein that estrogen binds to in order to do its work–is deeply ancient. Joseph Thornton of the University of Chicago and his colleagues have estimated that it is around 1.2 billion to 600 million years old–roughly twice as old as the testosterone receptor. In addition to helping regulate the reproductive system, estrogen influences fine-motor control and memory, enhances the growth and development of neurons, and helps to prevent hardening of the arteries.

Important for the purposes of this discussion, estrogen also improves fat metabolism. During exercise, estrogen seems to encourage the body to use stored fat for energy before stored carbohydrates. Fat contains more calories per gram than carbohydrates do, so it burns more slowly, which can delay fatigue during endurance activity. Not only does estrogen encourage fat burning, but it also promotes greater fat storage within muscles–marbling if you will–which makes that fat's energy more readily available. Adiponectin, another hormone that is typically present in higher amounts in females than in males, further enhances fat metabolism while sparing carbohydrates for future use, and it protects muscle from breakdown. Anne Friedlander of Stanford University and her colleagues found that females use as much as 70 percent more fat for energy during exercise than males.

Correspondingly, the muscle fibers of females differ from those of males. Females have more type I, or "slow-twitch," muscle fibers than males do. These fibers generate energy slowly by using fat. They are not all that powerful, but they take a long time to become fatigued. They are the endurance muscle fibers. Males, in contrast, typically have more type II ("fast-twitch") fibers, which use carbohydrates to provide quick energy and a great deal of power but tire rapidly.

Females also tend to have a greater number of estrogen receptors on their skeletal muscles compared with males. This arrangement makes these muscles more sensitive to estrogen, including to its protective effect after physical activity. Estrogen's ability to increase fat metabolism and regulate the body's response to the hormone insulin can help prevent muscle breakdown during intense exercise.

Furthermore, estrogen appears to have a stabilizing effect on cell membranes that might otherwise rupture from acute stress brought on by heat and exercise. Ruptured cells release enzymes called creatine kinases, which can damage tissues.

Studies of females and males during and after exercise bolster these claims. Linda Lamont of the University of Rhode Island and her colleagues, as well as Michael Riddell of York University in Canada and his colleagues, found that females experienced less muscle breakdown than males after the same bouts of exercise. Tellingly, in a separate study, Mazen J. Hamadeh of York University and his colleagues found that males supplemented with estrogen suffered less muscle breakdown during cycling than those who didn't receive estrogen supplements. In a similar vein, research led by Ron Maughan of the University of St. Andrews in Scotland found that females were able to perform significantly more weight-lifting repetitions than males at the same percentages of their maximal strength.

If females are better able to use fat for sustained energy and keep their muscles in better condition during exercise, then they should be able to run greater distances with less fatigue relative to males. In fact, an analysis of marathons carried out by Robert Deaner of Grand Valley State University demonstrated that females tend to slow down less as a race progresses compared with males.

If you follow long-distance races, you might be thinking, wait—males are outperforming females in endurance events! But this is only sometimes the case. Females are more regularly dominating ultraendurance events such as the more than 260-mile Montane Spine foot race through England and Scotland, the 21-mile swim across the English Channel and the 4,300-mile Trans Am cycling race across the U.S. Sometimes female athletes compete in these races while attending to the needs of their children. In 2018 English runner Sophie Power ran the 105-mile Ultra-Trail du Mont-Blanc race in the Alps while still breastfeeding her three-month-old at rest stations.

Inequity between male and female athletes is a result not of inherent biological differences between the sexes but of biases in how they are treated in sports. As an example, some endurance-running events allow the use of professional runners called pacesetters to help competitors perform their best. Men are not permitted to act as pacesetters in many women's events because of the belief that they will make the women "artificially faster," as though women were not actually doing the running themselves.

The modern physiological evidence, along with historical examples, exposes deep flaws in the idea that physical inferiority prevented females from partaking in hunting during our evolutionary past. The evidence from prehistory further undermines this notion.

Consider the skeletal remains of ancient people. Differences in body size between females and males of a species, a phenomenon called sexual size dimorphism, correlate with social structure. In species with pronounced size dimorphism, larger males compete with one another for access to females, and among the great apes larger males socially dominate females. Low sexual size dimorphism is characteristic of egalitarian and monogamous species. Modern humans have low sexual size dimorphism compared with the other great apes. The same goes for human ancestors spanning the past two million years, suggesting that the social structure of humans changed from that of our chimpanzeelike ancestors.

Anthropologists also look at damage on our ancestors' skeletons for clues to their behavior. Neandertals are the best-studied extinct members of the human family because we have a rich fossil record of their remains. Neandertal females and males do not differ in their trauma patterns, nor do they exhibit sex differences in pathology from repetitive actions. Their skeletons show the same patterns of wear and tear. This finding suggests that they were doing the same things, from ambush-hunting large game animals to processing hides for leather. Yes, Neandertal women were spearing woolly rhinoceroses, and Neandertal men were making clothing.

Males living in the Upper Paleolithic—the cultural period between roughly 45,000 and 10,000 years ago, when early modern humans entered Europe—do show higher rates of a set of injuries to the right elbow region known as thrower's elbow, which could mean they were more likely than females to throw spears. But it does not mean women were not hunting, because this period is also when people invented the bow and arrow, hunting nets and fishing hooks. These more sophisticated tools enabled humans to catch a wider variety of animals; they were also easier on hunters' bodies. Women may have favored hunting tactics that took advantage of these new technologies.

What is more, females and males were buried in the same way in the Upper Paleolithic. Their bodies were interred with the same kinds of artifacts, or grave goods, suggesting that the groups they lived in did not have social hierarchies based on sex.

Ancient DNA provides additional clues about social structure and potential gender roles in ancestral human communities. Patterns of variation in the Y chromosome, which is paternally inherited, and in mitochondrial DNA, which is maternally inherited, can reveal differences in how males and females dispersed after reaching maturity. Thanks to analyses of DNA extracted from fossils, we now know of three Neandertal groups that engaged in patrilocality—wherein males were more likely to stay in the group they were born into and females moved to other groups—although we do not know how widespread this practice was.

Patrilocality is believed to have been an attempt to avoid incest by trading potential mates with other groups. Nevertheless, many Neandertals show both genetic and anatomical evidence of repeated inbreeding in their ancestry. They lived in small, nomadic groups with low population densities and endured frequent local extinctions, which produced much lower levels of genetic diversity than we see in living humans. This is probably why we don't see any evidence in their skeletons of sex-based differences in behavior.

For those practicing a foraging subsistence strategy in small family groups, flexibility and adaptability are much more important than rigid roles, gendered or otherwise. Individuals get injured or die, and the availability of animal and plant foods changes with the seasons. All group members need to be able to step into any role depending on the situation, whether that role is hunter or breeding partner.

Observations of recent and contemporary foraging societies provide direct evidence of women participating in hunting. The most cited examples come from the Agta people of the Philippines. Agta women hunt while menstruating, pregnant and breastfeeding, and they have the same hunting success as Agta men.

They are hardly alone. A recent study of ethnographic data spanning the past 100 years—much of which was ignored by Man the Hunter contributors—found that women from a wide range of cultures hunt animals for food. Abigail Anderson and Cara Wall-Scheffler, both then at Seattle Pacific University, and their colleagues reported that 79 percent of the 63 foraging societies with clear descriptions of their hunting strategies feature women hunters. The women participate in hunting regardless of their childbearing status. These findings directly challenge the Man the Hunter assumption that women's bodies and childcare responsibilities limit their efforts to gathering foods that cannot run away.

So much about female exercise physiology and the lives of prehistoric women remains to be discovered. But the idea that in the past men were hunters and women were not is absolutely unsupported by the limited evidence we have. Female physiology is optimized for exactly the kinds of endurance activities involved in procuring game animals for food. And ancient women and men appear to have engaged in the same foraging activities rather than upholding a sex-based division of labor. It was the arrival some 10,000 years ago of agriculture, with its intensive investment in land, population growth and resultant clumped resources, that led to rigid gendered roles and economic inequality.

Now when you think of "cave people," we hope, you will imagine a mixed-sex group of hunters encircling an errant reindeer or knapping stone tools together rather than a heavy-browed man with a club over one shoulder and a trailing bride. Hunting may have been remade as a masculine activity in recent times, but for most of human history, it belonged to everyone.

About the Authors

Cara Ocobock studies human biology at the University of Notre Dame. A former powerlifter, she explores the physiological and behavioral mechanisms necessary to cope with and adapt to extreme climates and high levels of physical activity.

Sarah Lacy is a biological anthropologist at the University of Delaware. She studies the oral and respiratory health differences between Neandertals and early modern humans. Lacy is also a trained doula and an advocate for safer pregnancy and birth in the U.S.

Why We Believe the Myth of High Crime Rates

By Sara Novak

Americans are convinced that they are living in a world ravaged by crime. In major cities, we fear riding public transportation or going out after dark. We buy weapons for self-defense and skip our nightly jogs. Next to the weather, the explosion of crime is a favorite topic of conversation. The overwhelming consensus is that crime is only getting worse. According to a Gallup poll, in late 2022, 78 percent of Americans contended that there was more crime than there used to be.

These perceptions would make sense if they were accurate, but they aren't. Crime, in fact, is down in the U.S., rivaling low levels that haven't been seen since the 1960s. According to FBI data, violent crime rates dropped by 8 percent and property crime dropped by about 6 percent by the third quarter of last year, compared with the same period in 2022. Still, the reality of these optimistic statistics doesn't quell people's fears.

New York City is a prime example. Crime was down by 6 percent in July 2023 from a year earlier. Specifically, murder was down by 11 percent, rape was down by 11 percent, and robbery was down by 6 percent. Yet at the time that these statistics were released in 2023, a poll of New Yorkers' feelings around crime painted a grim picture of a city riddled with violence. The poll found that 61 percent of New Yorkers were worried about being the target of crime and that 36 percent fretted about the safety of public places. It is true that crime increased during the pandemic, and revising the way we view public safety after such a spike in crime statistics has ended happens at a slow pace. The pandemic is a case in point. The figures on major crime perceptions have remained inflated for years.

The reasons for such misperceptions are manifold. Crime tends to concentrate in certain places, mostly within poorer neighborhoods in cities such as Baltimore, New Orleans, Detroit, Birmingham, Ala., and Memphis, Tenn. This means that most of us will never experience it. Only 2 percent of people are ever affected by violent crime, and 15 percent are affected by any type of misconduct. Perceptions matter because in most cases, they are the sole basis for the fears that fuel the idea that crime is rampant. That can affect people in different ways. The older you are, for example, the more likely you are to fear crime even though you're half as likely to ever experience it, compared with other age groups.

Even more surprisingly, if you live in a part of the country with little crime, you're probably more frightened of it than people who actually live in the relatively few neighborhoods where it is commonplace, such as the Belmont neighborhood in Detroit or Hopkins–Middle East in Baltimore, where violent crimes are respectively 150 and 300 times more likely to happen, compared with other neighborhoods. A study published in the April 2018 issue of the journal Humanities and Social Sciences Communications found that "significant levels of fear are often reported by people who enjoy low levels of victimization." Study co-author Steven Bishop, a social science expert at University College London, says that if you experience crime or the threat of it more often, you're more likely to have adjusted your fears in line with reality. In neighborhoods with more crime, people harness their expectations and avoid the areas where criminals congregate. But when you're never exposed to crime, you're a poor judge of the risk of encountering it.

Oftentimes, our perceptions of crime are built around an imaginary "elsewhere" in which, in the most extreme scenario, civil order has collapsed, says Wesley G. Skogan, a professor of crime policy and the politics of crime at Northwestern University. When we're asked about our own neighborhood, for example, we're more likely to be moderately realistic about crime levels, compared with when we're asked about other parts of the country. "Within your neighborhood, you're talking about your own experiences and the experiences of those whom you know," Skogan says. In other words, your own insights into levels of public safety are the most accurate.

There are many reasons for these attitudes. Partisanship plays a growing role in fueling these perspectives. Our perspectives on crime are shaped by the politics of the moment—and have been for some time. During both George H.W. Bush's and Bill Clinton's presidencies, opposing parties held similar views on crime. But around 2000, perspectives began to depend on who was in power. According to the 2022 Gallup Poll, with President Joe Biden in the White House, 73 percent of Republicans said crime in their area was growing while only 42 percent of Democrats agreed. "Crime has become a big partisan split with the biggest gap in history happening during the Biden administration," says Skogan. What's more, Republicans are also more likely to be somewhat older, which could be a factor contributing to their fear of crime. (The average Republican is 50 years old, while the average Democrat is 47.)

Watershed events such as September 11 also contribute to how we think about crime. According to John Roman, director of the Center on Public Safety & Justice at NORC at the University of Chicago, the 9/11 attacks marked a period under the George W. Bush administration when our views about crime began to fall out of line with reality. Roman contends that, as a nation, we didn't foresee the largest terrorist attack in our country's history, and that makes us worry that even when crime statistics show a reduction, an unforeseen event may still strike without warning. "Ever since 9/11 we've been bombarded with warnings and messages that didn't exist before," Roman says. Every time you're in an airport or train station, there are warning signs that say things like "if you see something, say something"—reminders that lead to hypervigilance.

After 9/11 the federal government took on a partial role as public safety overseer, instituting a color-coded warning system to alert us to pending terrorist attacks. But that warning system is gone—and according to Roman, people have been left to make their own judgments about what it means to be safe, which can translate into the feeling of having to be on guard all the time. Similar issues arise when changes are made in policing. More and more cities have the police patrol with their lights flashing; while the goal is to raise police visibility, that tactic can result in the opposite of its intended effect.

Additionally, features that create a sense of disorder within a given neighborhood—for example, graffiti, broken-down buildings and trash—are often wrongly associated with an increased risk of crime. According to a September 2023 study published in the journal *Landscape and Urban Planning*, "public space regeneration significantly improves safety perceptions for both genders." Seeing drug use in public places, graffiti and people sleeping on public transportation all send psychological warning signs to the average person who's just trying to get home from work. Still, it's largely inaccurate messaging, in Roman's view. "Disorder and danger really aren't as highly correlated as people think," he says.

Media reports contribute to these flawed perceptions. Crimes that happen halfway across the globe have no real impact on our personal experience of safety on the street but can still weigh heavily on our psyche, Bishop says. This is also true for social media. "Overall, media and social media influenced perceptions of how frequently crime occurs," reported a September 2017 study published in the *American International Journal of Social Science*.

Pablo Navarrete Hernandez of the University of Sheffield in England, lead author of the 2023 *Landscape and Urban Planning* study, says that misplaced fears have been shown to have a major impact on perceptions about the neighborhoods in which we live and how public resources are allocated to them. Spending on police for neighborhoods with relatively low crime rates can divert expenditures from needier areas.

Misperceptions also affect those who end up alone and indoors because of fears of nonexistent crime. Parents may be afraid to take their kids to the park or on walks around the neighborhood. Fears of taking the metro or the bus may keep us at home. And older people may forgo their favorite hobbies and social contacts, contributing to the national epidemic of loneliness and the health risks that come with it. In the end, fear begins to hold us hostage much more than the risk of crime ever could.

About the Author

Sara Novak is a science writer based on Sullivan's Island, S.C. Her work has appeared in Discover, Sierra Magazine, Popular Science, New Scientist, *and more. Follow Novak on X (formerly Twitter) @sarafnovak*

The Myth that Musicians Die at 27 Shows How Superstitions Are Made

By Rachel Nuwer

Zackary Dunivin, a sociologist now at the University of California, Davis, was watching a movie about artist Jean-Michel Basquiat when something in the epilogue caught his attention. Basquiat, the explanatory text stated, died of a drug overdose at the age of 27. Dunivin felt that something about this particular age seemed to lend additional weight to the tragedy of Basquiat's death, and he quickly realized why: Basquiat was a member of the "27 Club." This widespread myth holds that famous people, especially musicians, are unusually likely to die at age 27.

The film, *Basquiat*, made Dunivin wonder about how the 27 Club myth propagates itself and what that means for the people who are caught up in it. In a new *Proceedings of the National Academy of Sciences USA* paper, he provides some answers: more attention is paid to people who die at the age of 27 because of the existence of the club, he found, and this creates a positive feedback loop that both strengthens the legend's potency and the fame of those it pertains to.

"The weird thing about this particular myth is: even if you don't know about the 27 Club, you encounter more famous dead people who died at 27," Dunivin says. "We've made this myth appear to be true because the appearance that more people who die at 27 is real."

The idea that especially talented people are prone to untimely deaths goes back to ancients. As noted by the Greek playwright Menander in the Fourth Century B.C.E., "Whom the gods love die young."

The idea that musicians, artists, actors and other creative people are more likely to die specifically at the age of 27, however, emerged more recently, after a series of high-profile deaths in the early 1970s. Between 1969 and 1971, Brian Jones, Jimi Hendrix, Janis Joplin and Jim Morrison each died at that age. By chance, these rock stars were all icons of the counterculture movement, and the first and last of their deaths occurred two years apart to the day. "We are meaning-making machines–that's what we do as human beings," Dunivin says. "You look at that and say, 'It can't be a coincidence!'"

The fact that people latched on to this particular group of deaths in the 1970s is somewhat justified, Dunivin continues, because of just how unusual it was. In the new paper, he calculated a steep one in 100,000 chance that four 27-year-olds at the top of a Wikipedia list of famous people–the list's 99.9th percentile, "true superstars," as Dunivin says–would die in a two-year period.

The myth's popularity has been revived and reinforced over the years, he adds, by other headline-making deaths of famous 27-year-olds, including Kurt Cobain and Amy Winehouse.

Dunivin did not set out to debunk the myth itself–that had already been done by another group of researchers in 2011. Instead he wanted to untangle how a legend that emerged out of a random but "truly strange" series of events went on to have a real-world impact by shaping the legacies of other famous people who subsequently died at 27.

For the data, Dunivin and his co-author, sociologist Patrick Kaminski of Indiana University Bloomington and the University of Stuttgart in Germany, turned to a database of notable people that includes nearly everyone with a Wikipedia page in all languages. They limited their analysis to people who were born after 1900 and who died before 2015, leaving them with 344,156 individuals. The researchers used page visits as a proxy for fame.

Statistical models that they used reconfirmed that there is no increased risk of famous people dying at age 27. Among those in the 90th percentile of fame and higher, however, those who died at 27 did experience an extra boost in popularity that could not be accounted for by other factors. The effect was particularly pronounced for the most famous of the famous, or individuals who roughly achieved the 99th percentile of fame. That bump indicates that people who die at age 27 "are considerably more likely to be more famous" than those who die at 26 or 28, Dunivin says.

Cultural myths are generally "very hard to study empirically," says Omar Lizardo, a sociologist at the University of California,

Los Angeles, who was not involved in the work. But by using a "clever" approach, he says, Dunivin and Kaminski did "a good job of providing a lot of circumstantial evidence that the phenomenon is real and that artists who die around that age garner more attention and notoriety."

Timothy Tangherlini, a folklorist at the University of California, Berkeley, who was not involved in the research, calls it a "major contribution" to what is known as computational folklore.

The authors succeed in "leveraging sophisticated statistical models and novel data to understand the feedback mechanisms of belief, storytelling and their real-world effects," Tangherlini says. "Ultimately, they provide a mechanism for understanding how, in death, these young musicians–because of an unusual coincidence of timing–have grown in fame because of the emergence of a coordinating narrative that clearly resonated among fans and the broader public."

About the Author

Rachel Nuwer is a science journalist and author. Her latest book is I Feel Love: MDMA and the Quest for Connection in a Fractured World *(Bloomsbury, 2023). Follow her on X @RachelNuwer*

Section 7: In My Humble Opinion

We Can Live without Fossil Fuels

By Naomi Oreskes

The final results are not yet in, but it's pretty certain that 2024 is going to be the hottest year on record. Practically every week this year, we heard of some new daily or monthly record being broken, some extreme weather event made more extreme than it would have been by human-caused climate change. In July exceptional rainfall led to flooding that triggered deadly landslides in the Kerala region of India, killing hundreds of people. In September, Hurricane Helene became one of the biggest storms to hit the U.S. Fueled by record-high ocean temperatures, the storm brought torrential rains and massive storm surges to the Southeast. At press time, the death toll from the hurricane had surpassed 230.

Sadly, reports of these events often provoke not shock, sadness or outrage but rather a sense of déjà vu, if not ennui. If 2024 does prove to be the hottest year ever measured, it will be the fifth time in less than a decade that we have faced such a grim fact. Perhaps for this reason, the response of the fossil-fuel industry is to shrug its shoulders and insist that, despite all the climate damage that fossil fuels cause, we just can't live without them. In a white paper published earlier this year, KinderMorgan, which owns and operates pipelines, put it this way: "There is an enduring economic and social need for fossil fuels that will continue to play a central role in our lives." ExxonMobil's 2024 Global Outlook declares that "oil and natural gas remain vital" because they are "needed for modern life."

Everyone involved in the energy and environment conversation knows any transition away from fossil fuels and toward renewable energy will take time. Indeed, this is why it's so consequential that the oil and gas industry has worked for decades to delay the transition, which even it now acknowledges is necessary.

The argument that we can't live without a dangerous, even deadly product is an old one. In their new book on the history of health disparities in the U.S. (and the role of corporate America in creating and reinforcing many of those disparities), historians David Rosner and Gerald Markowitz recount an argument made 99 years ago, when the fossil-fuel industry defended an activity that would soon kill large numbers of people: putting lead in gasoline.

By the 1920s many people, most notably American physician and Harvard University professor Alice Hamilton, had become concerned about occupational exposure to toxic materials, such as lead, asbestos and mercury. Hamilton was an expert on lead poisoning, and some states had passed laws to limit exposure to toxic substances in the workplace, in part based on her work. When the oil industry decided to add lead to gasoline, Hamilton was concerned. The situation pitted her against some of the biggest names in American business, including industrialists Charles F. Kettering and Alfred P. Sloan and oil magnate John D. Rockefeller.

General Motors engineer Thomas Midgley, Jr., had discovered that adding tetraethyl lead to gasoline solved the problem of knocking–the noise caused by fuel burning unevenly or incompletely in an engine. Midgley worked under Kettering–GM's head of research–who reported directly to Sloan, GM's CEO. GM quickly contracted with Rockefeller's Standard Oil to put tetraethyl lead into gasoline. By 1923 the product was on the market.

But there was a catch. It had been known since classical antiquity that lead is highly toxic; Midgley himself had suffered a bout of lead poisoning as a result of his research. Many workers in industrial settings where lead was used became ill or died. So GM and DuPont–which would manufacture the tetraethyl lead–agreed the product would be marketed simply as "ethyl."

It didn't take long for scientists to voice concerns. According to Rosner and Markowitz, the U.S. surgeon general wrote to the chair of DuPont asking whether the companies had taken public health impacts into account. Midgley admitted that neither DuPont nor GM had collected any relevant data, but he nonetheless insisted that the amounts that an ordinary person would be exposed to would be harmless.

In 1925 the surgeon general organized a conference of businesspeople, union leaders, scientists, doctors and government officials to consider the matter. Given what Midgley told the surgeon general, one might expect the representatives of American industry to have insisted that lead in gasoline was safe. Instead they argued it was essential for the U.S. economy, for industrial progress, for the American way of life.

Kettering contended that because oil supplies were limited, anything that improved efficiency had to be viewed as indispensable. Standard Oil's lawyers and engineers stated at the conference: "Our continued development of motor fuels is essential in our civilization."

In later years, industry representatives and defenders would repeatedly reprise this theme. True, some workers got sick or even died, but this was the price of progress. The editor of the journal *Chemical and Metallurgical Engineering* asserted that "casualties" from lead "were negligible compared to human sacrifice in the development of many other industrial enterprises."

In 1965 California Institute of Technology geochemist Clair C. Patterson estimated that the blood lead level of many Americans was more than 100 times what it would be from natural causes and well above what was known to cause at least low-level lead poisoning. Meanwhile other scientific studies were proving that even low levels of lead exposure could cause neurotoxicity, with alarming effects on intelligence and behavior. In 1973 the U.S. began a gradual phaseout of leaded gasoline. In 2021 Algeria became the last country to ban it.

When lead was removed from gas, the positive effects were dramatic. One study found that between 1976 and 1995, mean American blood lead levels dropped 90 percent. Moreover, the scaremongering predictions of Midgley and Co. did not come true. Not only did the American economy not collapse when leaded gasoline for cars was phased out, but it took only a few short years for car manufacturers to redesign engines to operate with unleaded gas. Leaded gasoline was not essential to civilization, and neither are fossil fuels. What is essential to civilization is that we dramatically reduce our use of coal, oil and gas—the largest contributors to the existential threat of global climate change—and thereby set our planet on a path toward a safer future.

This is an opinion and analysis article, and the views expressed by the author or authors are not necessarily those of Scientific American.

About the Author

Naomi Oreskes is a professor of the history of science at Harvard University. She is author of Why Trust Science? *(Princeton University Press, 2019) and co-author of* The Big Myth *(Bloomsbury, 2023).*

Challenging Big Oil's Big Lie about Plastic Recycling

By Judith Enck

Among the plastic in your house might be an orange-colored hard laundry detergent bottle and a squeezable clear ketchup bottle. Come recycling day, you might put them on the curb in a blue bin or bag, expecting they will become something new.

But here's the problem: those two plastic bottles cannot be recycled together because they are different colors, different plastic types and made from different chemicals. Unlike an old aluminum can that can be recycled into a new aluminum can, plastics are fundamentally not designed to be recycled.

Yet the idea that plastics are just as recyclable as aluminum is a pervasive misconception because the plastics and petrochemical industries have been drilling it into our brains for nearly half a century. This long con has allowed these industries to make billions of dollars with zero accountability–until recently, when California attorney general Rob Bonta announced that the state of California was suing ExxonMobil for environmental damage and recycling lies.

This is a historic moment in the fight against plastic pollution, a crisis that has been created by companies that have known recycling was not possible for most plastics. While others have filed important suits against consumer brand companies for their pollution, like New York attorney general Letitia James' lawsuit against PepsiCo, Bonta's suit is the first to target a company for lying about plastic recycling's efficacy.

Exxon, one of the largest oil and gas companies in the world, was an obvious company to focus on. Americans typically associate the company with gas stations, but Exxon also makes the polymers–the chains of repeating chemical pieces–that become plastic bottles, cups, utensils, takeout containers and other packaging for U.S. consumer goods. It considers the manufacturing of plastic components a "core" part of its business and, according to Bonta's lawsuit, sees 80 percent of the company's growth potential as "dependent on single-use plastics applications."

Think about that: while you're stressing about what to put in the recycling bin, companies like Exxon are on a mission to find new ways to pump unnecessary plastic into the world.

The composition of most plastic makes it an inherently unrecyclable material. More than 16,000 chemicals are used to make different plastics to give the material qualities like color and flexibility, with different types of plastic using different combinations of these additives. The small amount of plastic that is actually recyclable (primarily No. 1 and No. 2, PET and HDPE) is delivered to a facility where the plastic is shredded and ground. Unlike paper, which can be turned into new paper products several times, recycled plastic typically becomes plastic lumber or clothing–which then can no longer be recycled and does not biodegrade.

That's why less than 6 percent of plastics are recycled in the U.S. and why it's deceptive that Exxon and others have spent millions over decades on public relations campaigns that falsely promote plastic recycling's ability to manage all of the mess.

According to the California attorney general, this is illegal. Bonta's lawsuit extensively outlines the company's deception and includes a statement from an Exxon employee from 1994 saying, "We are committed to the activities but not committed to the results," when discussing plastic recycling projects.

This distraction technique was meant to shift the blame and responsibility for plastic pollution from companies to consumers while companies exponentially increased the amount of plastic being produced. And it worked. Today, there isn't a place on Earth untouched by plastic. It's been found in Arctic sea ice, the deepest part of the ocean, the remotest mountains, in much of our food, and in our bodies. Plastic doesn't biodegrade; it breaks up into smaller pieces. This chokes wildlife, enters the air we breathe and finds its way into the water we drink. This toxic material, often used for just a moment, ends up polluting the environment for centuries.

Exxon and others are now reusing the same distraction technique to promote what they call "advanced recycling," a process that uses high heat to turn plastic into small amounts of fuel or uses often toxic chemicals to attempt to make new plastics. Like mechanical recycling, it's been unsuccessful for decades.

Today only nine chemical recycling facilities exist in the U.S., and even if they were operating at full capacity–which they are not–they would handle less than 1.2 percent of U.S. plastic waste. These facilities create a new universe of environmental problems, such as toxic contamination and air pollution, and they continue the hoax of plastics recycling. Most of these facilities are located in low-income communities and communities of color.

Bonta's lawsuit will hold Exxon accountable for its disinformation around advanced recycling in addition to traditional recycling–another unprecedented and laudable move. "ExxonMobil has known that mechanical recycling, and now 'advanced recycling,' will never be able to process more than a tiny fraction of the waste it produces," the lawsuit says.

This lawsuit stands on the shoulders of cases brought by state attorneys general against tobacco companies in the 1980s. It has two similar goals as the successful tobacco lawsuits: stop the deception and address the damages. When California wins this case, ExxonMobil and the trade associations it funds will have to stop lying about plastics recycling. Additionally, Exxon will be required to put millions of dollars into an abatement fund that will enable California to address the plague of plastic pollution.

Companies like Exxon have long used their power and money to evade consequences for the devastation fueled by their own greed. It takes leaders like Attorney General Bonta to change that.

This legal action sets a precedent for other state attorneys general to follow. As the litigation piles up on big oil for climate liability, smart companies can reduce their legal exposure by telling the truth about plastics and plastics recycling. It's not only the right thing to do; it's also what the law requires.

This is an opinion and analysis article, and the views expressed by the author or authors are not necessarily those of Scientific American.

About the Author

Judith Enck is a former EPA regional administrator, the president of Beyond Plastics and a professor at Bennington College.

Many Older People Maintain and Even Gain Cognitive Skills

By Lydia Denworth

As I watched my parents' generation reach their 80s, I was struck by the dramatic differences among them. A handful suffered from dementia, but many others remained cognitively sharp—even if their knees and hips didn't quite keep up with the speed of their thoughts.

That observation runs counter to prejudices about aging, which were highlighted early in the 2024 presidential race between elderly candidates, but these biases permeate society in general. "The belief about old people is that they're all kind of the same, they're doddering, and that aging is this steady downward slope," says psychologist Laura Carstensen, founding director of the Stanford Center on Longevity. That view, she says, is a great misunderstanding.

Instead research highlights the very differences I noticed. In our 40s, most people are cognitively similar. Divergences in cognition appear around age 60. By 80 "it's quite dramatically splayed out," says physician John Rowe, a professor of health policy and aging at Columbia University's Mailman School of Public Health. Yes, there will be a group diminished by dementia and cognitive decline, but in general the 80-somethings "include the wisest people on the planet," Carstensen says.

Focusing on only those with poor brain health misses more than half the population. Rowe led research showing that in the six years after turning 75, about half of people showed little to no change in their physical, biological, hormonal and cognitive functioning, whereas the other half changed quite a lot. A longer-term study followed more than 2,000 individuals with an average age of 77 for up to 16 years. It showed that the three quarters who did not develop dementia showed little to no cognitive decline.

Some of this is related to genetics. Studies of successful aging have shown that genes account for 30 to 50 percent of physical and cognitive changes. But factors like a healthy way of life and good self-esteem are also consequential. So to an extent, Rowe says, "this is really good news because it means that you are, in fact, in control of your old age."

Research has also busted the myth that there is no upside to aging past 70 or so. "We have found very clearly that there are things that improve with age," Rowe says. The ability to resolve conflicts strengthens, for instance. Aging is also associated with more positive overall emotional well-being, which means older adults are more emotionally stable than younger adults, as well as better at regulating desires.

The normal aging process does bring changes to the brain, says Denise Park, a neuroscientist at the University of Texas at Dallas. There is some shrinkage in the frontal lobes and some damage to neurons and their connections. Cognitive processing slows down. Yet that slowdown is usually on the order of milliseconds and doesn't always make a meaningful difference in daily life. And to compensate, older people activate more of the brain for tasks such as reading. "Older adults will often forge additional pathways" for particular activities, Park says. "Those pathways may not be as efficient as the pathways that younger adults use, but they nonetheless work."

The cliché that age brings wisdom is also backed up by science. "Where older adults really shine is in their knowledge," Park says. If you think of the brain as a computer, "there's a lot more on the hard disk," she says. Older adults can draw on their experience and often have much better solutions to problems than younger adults. "Frequently that can give them an edge that is unexpected," Park says.

That edge shows up in decision-making and conflict resolution. One study asked several hundred people to read stories about personal and group conflicts. The study, published in 2010 in the *Proceedings of the National Academy of Sciences USA*, found that participants older than 60 were more likely to emphasize multiple perspectives, to compromise, and to recognize the limits of one's own knowledge. Carstensen's observations reinforce these conclusions. "The decisions that people make as they get older tend to be ones that take into consideration multiple factors and multiple stakeholders," she says. Older adults are less likely than younger people to see the world in stark black-and-white terms. Carstensen says that when responses in such studies are rated by observers who don't know how old participants are, the older people's answers are seen as wiser.

Such wisdom may be the result of a gradual shift in perspective, Carstensen says. As we age and become more aware that time is short, we focus more on the positive. A meta-analysis combining data on more than 7,000 older adults found they were significantly more likely than younger adults to lean toward the positive versus the negative when processing information.

The COVID pandemic has showcased this contrast. In a 2020 survey of nearly 1,000 adults, Carstensen and her colleagues found that the older adults were better able to cope with the stresses of the pandemic, despite being one of the groups at highest risk of health complications and death.

The fact is that different parts of the body can age at different rates in the same person. Someone who stumbles on stairs may do so because of creaky knees, not cognitive decline. If someone has a healthy brain, age alone might be considered a definite asset. "If you were to take the kinds of decisions presidents make and compare them to the kinds of skills older people have versus younger people, I put my money on older people," Carstensen says.

This is an opinion and analysis article, and the views expressed by the author or authors are not necessarily those of Scientific American.

About the Author

Lydia Denworth is an award-winning science journalist and contributing editor for Scientific American. *She is author of* Friendship *(W. W. Norton, 2020).*

GLOSSARY

anthropomorphize To attribute human form or personality to things that are not human.

anti-vaxxer A person who opposes the use of some or all vaccines, regulations mandating vaccination, or usually both.

arbitrary Existing or coming about seemingly at random or by chance.

bias To have a settled and often prejudiced outlook on something.

conception A general idea.

consensus General agreement.

debunk To expose the falseness of a claim.

dimorphism The existence of two different forms (as of color or size) of a species especially in the same population.

dominance Controlling, prevailing, or powerful position especially in a social hierarchy.

entrepreneur An individual who creates a business.

Faustian bargain Made or done for present gain without regard for future cost or consequences.

huckster One who sells or advertises something in an aggressive, dishonest, or annoying way.

hypothesis A tentative assumption made in order to draw out and test its logical or empirical consequences.

magnetoencephalography A noninvasive technique that detects and records the magnetic field associated with electrical activity in the brain.

meme An amusing or interesting item (such as a captioned picture or video) or genre of items that is spread widely online, especially through social media.

misconstrue To interpret (something, such as a statement or action) wrongly.

nuanced Having or characterized by subtle and often appealingly complex qualities, aspects, or distinctions (as in character or tone).

omnipotent Having virtually unlimited authority or influence.

proboscideans Any of an order *(Proboscidea)* of large mammals comprising the elephants and extinct related forms (such as mastodons).

reverence Honor or respect that is either felt or shown.

smoking gun Something that serves as conclusive evidence or proof (as of a crime or scientific theory).

spectrophotometer A photometer for measuring the relative intensities of the light in different parts of a spectrum.

stereotype Something conforming to a fixed or general pattern (especially a standardized mental picture that is held in common by members of a group and that represents an oversimplified opinion, prejudiced attitude, or uncritical judgment).

sustainability Of, relating to, or being a method of harvesting or using a resource so that the resource is not depleted or permanently damaged.

unassailable Not liable to doubt, attack, or question.

FURTHER INFORMATION

"5 Common Myths about the Brain," *Scientific American*, January 1, 2015, www.scientificamerican.com/article/5-common-myths-about-the-brain/.

Scudellari, Megan. "The Science Myths That Will Not Die," *Nature*, vol. 528, no. 7582, Dec. 2015, pp. 322–325, www.nature.com/news/the-science-myths-that-will-not-die-1.19022, https://doi.org/10.1038/528322a.

Reichelt, Amy. "No, Sugar Doesn't Make Your Kids Hyperactive," *The Conversation*, 28 May 2024, theconversation.com/no-sugar-doesnt-make-your-kids-hyperactive-229107.

"The Turkey-Tryptophan Connection—Is It Really What's behind the Thanksgiving Snooze?" Texas Health, October 24, 2023. www.texashealth.org/areyouawellbeing/Eating-Right/The-Turkey-Tryptophan-Connection-Is-It-Really-Whats-Behind-the-Thanksgiving-Snooze.

Osborne, Margaret. "Does Vanilla Flavoring Actually Come from Beaver Butts?" *Smithsonian Magazine*, November 21, 2023. www.smithsonianmag.com/smart-news/does-vanilla-flavoring-actually-come-from-beaver-butts-180983288/.

Wolchover, Natalie, and Life's Little Mysteries. "Could a Penny Dropped off a Skyscraper Actually Kill You?" *Scientific American*, March 5, 2012. www.scientificamerican.com/article/could-a-penny-dropped-off/.

Richards, Paul. "How Far Can Sharks Smell Blood?" *Field and Stream*, October 23, 2023. www.fieldandstream.com/survival/how-far-can-sharks-smell-blood.

Stromberg, Joseph. "It's a Myth: There's No Evidence That Coffee Stunts Kids' Growth," *Smithsonian Magazine*, December 20, 2013, www.smithsonianmag.com/science-nature/its-a-myth-theres-no-evidence-that-coffee-stunts-kids-growth-180948068/.

Lilienfeld, Scott O., Steven Jay Lynn, John Ruscio, and Barry L. Beyerstein. "Busting Big Myths in Popular Psychology," *Scientific American*, March 1, 2010. www.scientificamerican.com/article/busting-big-myths/.

Veneziano, Gabriele. "The Myth of the Beginning of Time," *Scientific American*, February 1, 2006. www.scientificamerican.com/article/the-myth-of-the-beginning-of-time-2006-02.

Mayo Clinic Staff. "Debunking COVID-19 (Coronavirus) Myths," Mayo Clinic, November 7, 2023. www.mayoclinic.org/diseases-conditions/coronavirus/in-depth/coronavirus-myths/art-20485720.

CITATIONS

1.1 Is the Alpha Wolf Idea a Myth? by Stephanie Pappas (February 28, 2023); 1.2 Males Aren't Larger Than Females in Most Mammalian Species by Rachel Nuwer (March 12, 2024); 1.3 Why Insects Are Lured to Lights in the Night by Gary Stix & Immy Smith (May 14, 2024); 1.4 Do Cats Really Hate Water? by Meghan Bartels (September 4, 2024); 1.5 'If Not Friend, Why Friend-Shaped?' A Beary Scientific Investigation by Carin Leong & Allison Parshall (June 6, 2024); 1.6 Do Animals Cry When They're Sad? by Hilde Vervaecke (March 1, 2024); 1.7 Fact or Fiction?: A Cockroach Can Live without Its Head by Charles Choi (March 15, 2007); 2.1 How Long Does It Really Take to Form a Habit? by Jocelyn Solis-Moreira (January 24, 2024); 2.2 Don't Fall for These Five Dangerous Tanning Myths by Riis Williams (May 31, 2024); 2.3 Do People Really Swallow 8 Spiders a Year While They Sleep? by Annie Sneed (April 15, 2014); 2.4 Crack Research: Good News about Knuckle Cracking by Steve Mirsky (December 1, 2009); 2.5 Your Body Has a Clever Way to Detect How Much Water You Should Drink Every Day by Claudia Wallis (Septembe 1, 2022); 2.6 Do We Really Use Only 10 Percent of Our Brains? by Barry L. Beyerstein (March 8, 2004); 2.7 The Adult Brain Does Grow New Neurons After All, Study Says by Karen Weintraub (March 25, 2019); Fact or Fiction?: If You Shave (or Wax), Your Hair Will Come Back Thicker by Dina Fine Maron (August 26, 2014); 3.1 Fact or Fiction?: South of the Equator Toilets Flush and Tornadoes Spin in the Opposite Direction by Robynne Boyd (June 28, 2007); 3.2 Mysterious Gamma-Ray Flashes May Be Missing Link for Lightning Bolts by Lee Billings (October 21, 2024); 3.3 Fact or Fiction?: If the Sky Is Green, Run for Cover—A Tornado Is Coming by Meredith Knight (June 14, 2007); 4.1 The Myth of Stephen Hawking by Charles Seife (April 6, 2021); 4.2 Fact or Fiction?: Mammoths Can Be Brought Back from Extinction by David Biello (June 10, 2014); 4.3 The Idea That a Scientific Theory Can Be 'Falsified' Is a Myth by Mano Singham (September 7, 2020); 4.4 Why Does the Moon Look Bigger Near the Horizon? by Phil Plait (October 18, 2024); 5.1 To Follow the Real Early Human Diet, Eat Everything by Kate Wong (June 25, 2024); 5.2 Fact or Fiction?: The 5-Second Rule for Dropped Food by Larry Greenemeier (March 25, 2014); 5.3 Fact or Fiction: Should You Feed a Cold and Starve a Fever? by Mark Fischetti (January 3, 2014); 5.4 Fact or Fiction: Raw Veggies are Healthier than Cooked Ones by Sushma Subramanian (March 31, 2009); 5.5 What the Evidence Says about Fluoride in Drinking Water by Saima S. Iqbal (November 27, 2024); 6.1 No, You Can't See the Great Wall of China from Space by Phil Plait (August 9, 2024); 6.2 Top 10 Myths about Sustainability by Michael D. Lemonick (March 1, 2009); 6.3 The Theory That Men Evolved to Hunt and Women Evolved to Gather Is Wrong by Cara Ocobock & Sarah Lacy (November 1, 2023); 6.4 Why We Believe the Myth of High Crime Rates by Sara Novak (April 11, 2024); The Myth that Musicians Die at 27 Shows How Superstitions Are Made by Rachel Nuwer (November 4, 2024); 7.1 We Can Live without Fossil Fuels by Naomi Oreskes (November 19, 2024); Challenging Big Oil's Big Lie about Plastic Recycling by Judith Enck (October 5, 2024); 7.3 Many Older People Maintain and Even Gain Cognitive Skills by Lydia Denworth (August 20, 2024).

Each author biography was accurate at the time the article was originally published.

INDEX